KEEPING OUR KIDS ALIVE

Parenting a
suicidal young person

DR LYN O'GRADY

AUSTRALIANACADEMICPRESS

First published 2020 by:
Australian Academic Press Group Pty. Ltd.
Samford Valley QLD, Australia
www.australianacademicpress.com.au

A catalogue record for this
book is available from the
NATIONAL LIBRARY OF AUSTRALIA
National Library of Australia

Keeping our kids alive: Parenting a suicidal young person.

ISBN   9781925644401 (paperback)
ISBN   9781925644418 (ebook)

Disclaimer
Every effort has been made in preparing this work to provide information based on accepted standards and practice at the time of publication. The publisher and author, however, make no representations or warranties with respect to the accuracy or completeness of the contents of this book and specifically disclaim any implied warranties of merchantability or fitness for a particular purpose. It is sold on the understanding that the publisher is not engaged in rendering professional services and neither the publisher nor the author shall be liable for damages arising herefrom. If professional advice or other expert assistance is required, the services of a competent professional should be sought.

Publisher: Stephen May
Copy Editor: Rhonda McPherson
Cover design: Luke Harris, Working Type Studio
Typesetting: Australian Academic Press
Printing: Lightning Source

Contents

A note regarding Aboriginal and Torres Strait Islander peoples vii

Acknowledgements viii

About the author..ix

Introduction..1

    The purpose of this book...6

    A quick note about language 7

    Talking to your teenager about this book 8

    How did you get here? 9

PART A   Understanding parenting and suicide 11

Chapter 1 — Being a parent of a teenager 15

    Parenting experiences..15

    Attachment 17

    Parenting styles 19

    Being a 'good enough' parent 21

    Reflection: The meaning of parenting to you..24

Chapter 2 — Teenage development...25

    Brain development and neuroscience...26

    Search for identity and meaning 27

    Importance of friends and belonging 32

    Where do parents fit in? 34

    Dependence and independence 38

    Reflection: Your teenagers' stage of development....................................39

Chapter 3 — What's different about being a parent of a teenager compared to a parent of a younger child?..........................41

Trust and confidentiality..........................42

Learning to let go..........................43

Values..........................44

Handling conflict..........................45

What caring looks like..........................47

The role of the school..........................48

Reflection: Making sense of parenting for you at the moment..........................50

Chapter 4 — Understanding suicide..........................51

Some theories about suicide..........................53

Chapter 5 — Suicide risk and protective factors and warning signs..........................61

Common myths about suicide..........................61

Risk and protective factors..........................61

Chapter 6 — What do we know about youth suicide?..........................69

What does research tell us about young people in Australia and suicide?..........................69

What might lead up to a suicide attempt by a young person?..........................70

What might this mean for your teenager?..........................78

Chapter 7 — Understanding suicide from a young person's perspective..........................81

Reflection Understanding suicide from a young person's perspective..........................90

Chapter 8 — The experience of being a parent of a teenager who is suicidal..........................91

PART B   Parenting a teenager who is suicidal..........................99

Chapter 9 — Safety first — managing the suicidal crisis..........................101

What might a crisis look like?..........................102

Seeking immediate help during a crisis..........................102

Types of help available..........................106

Assessments..........................109

Chapter 10 — Safety planning...111

    Safety planning and your role...115

Chapter 11 — Seeking ongoing help 119

    Communication and trust 120

    Plan for a return to school with support...............................123

    Role of families and friends 127

    Help your teenager continue to build their problem solving capacity 129

Chapter 12 — Mental health diagnoses and types of interventions 131

    Working with mental health professionals...........................131

    Getting a mental health diagnosis 135

    Getting an accurate diagnosis...145

    Treatments for suicidality..145

Chapter 13 — Self-care and seeking help for yourself....................149

    Dealing with feelings of shame and guilt............................156

    Facing fears 158

Chapter 14 — Family relationships...161

    Supporting the entire family unit 161

    The parenting relationship(s) 162

    Impact on sibling(s): their responses and needs 163

    Building resilience and deeper connections 164

    Importance of maintaining and strengthening relationships 165

    Harnessing key parenting skills 168

Chapter 15 — Tackling the underlying individual suicide risk factors 171

    Mental health problems...172

    Sense of self and self-worth...173

    Body image...176

    Sexuality...177

    Alcohol and other drugs...178

Technology use 180

Sleep 183

Chapter 16 — Tackling the broader social issues underlying suicide risk 185

Social relationships, including bullying and relationship break-ups...................185

Knowing someone who has died by suicide...187

Family relationships..188

School and study problems 190

Chapter 17 — Moving forward..193

Helping young people find meaning in life and hope for the future 193

Dealing with the present while looking forward 196

Being there when times get tough 198

Planning to get through tough times..199

Conclusion..203

Bibliography and further reading..205

Appendix A — What to do if your child is not yet a teenager 211

Appendix B — What to do if your child is a young adult...215

Appendix C — Useful resources 217

A note regarding Aboriginal and Torres Strait Islander peoples

Tragically a large proportion of children and young people who die by suicide in Australia are of Aboriginal and Torres Strait Islander ancestry. It is acknowledged that this book has limitations in this regard and is not intended to address the particular needs of Aboriginal and Torres Strait Islander families and communities. The author acknowledges the need for greater recognition and targeted resources to better understand and prevent suicides of young Aboriginals and Torres Strait Islanders.

Acknowledgements

A book like this can only be written because of the contributions of many people who often play unknowing roles behind the scenes. Firstly, to my parents, Kelvin, and Margaret (dec.), your encouragement to read and learn set me on a lifelong path towards a love of learning, research and knowledge translation. To my daughters, Laura and Caitlin, you taught me to learn about and value both childhood and parenthood. Even as adults, you both continue to teach and inspire me every day. My friends and work colleagues helped me to take the courageous step of writing this book. In particular, Harry Gelber and Alison Webb walked beside me every step of the way with encouragement. Thanks also to the parents and children I've worked with, and look forward to working with in the future, who entrusted me by sharing their family struggles. Finally, thanks to my publisher, Stephen May, for taking on the topic with sensitivity and providing the opportunity for this book to come to fruition.

About the author

Dr Lyn O'Grady, DPsych, MSuicidology, Grad Dip (Applied Psychology), BArts, is a registered Community Psychologist with a longstanding interest in the mental health of children, young people and families. She has worked with parents in community settings as well as with children and young people in school settings for over two decades. She served as the Australian Psychological Society's (APS) National Manager for *KidsMatter*, an Australian children's mental health initiative for early childhood services and schools, for six years. During this period, she was often called upon as the media spokesperson in relation to children's mental health for print and radio interviews. In 2019 she was the APS's spokesperson for the national Psychology Week promotion of their *Digital Me* Survey results, about the impact of social media on young people.

Lyn regularly presents at mental health conferences and is an accomplished facilitator of webinars on a range of mental health topics, reaching extensive numbers of health professionals through the national Mental Health Professionals Network. She delivered a series of webinars about suicide risk in early 2018 through the APS Institute and has co-authored a number of book chapters in international psychology handbooks and journal articles in the *Australian Community Psychologist*.

Introduction

I don't remember when I first heard about suicide. When I was a teenager, none of my school friends talked about hurting themselves or wanting to die. They could have been thinking about it for all I knew, but no one shared it with me. I now know, as a psychologist, that children and young people think about suicide, develop plans about how to kill themselves, and sometimes, tragically, even die by suicide. It was happening back then too. Just because something's not talked about doesn't mean it's not happening.

Suicide is a topic we're hearing a lot more about now and it's likely that even quite young children know about it. As parents, we need to be ready to not only have conversations about what suicide means but also to be open to the possibility that our children and teenagers may have suicidal thoughts and may act on them. Parenting forces us to confront issues with our kids that we won't always be ready for or want to know about. We tend to draw on our life experiences, but often having been teenagers ourselves isn't enough to help us feel confident and know what to do, especially when facing tough times.

We've recently been confronted with the Netflix series, *13 Reasons Why*. On watching the series, I was reminded of aspects of my own adolescence. These memories were juxtaposed against my more recent adult experience as a school psychologist. While the final episode initially showed the graphic depiction of death by suicide of the main character of Hannah, the rest of the episodes leading up to the finale highlighted many serious challenges faced by young people. The series was set in contemporary times in the

United States, based on a novel written by a male writer, Jay Asher, over 10 years ago, yet many of the issues facing Hannah and the other characters felt very real to me. The struggles of knowing who you are, wanting to fit in but struggling to know how, trying to find ways to understand complex feelings, wanting to voice concerns and views, but often not being heard even when finding the courage to speak up. The list of issues facing the characters goes on, and it's a very long list. As I watched the series, I was reminded again just how significant that life stage we call adolescence is. I recalled stories I'd heard from young people, families and health professionals I've worked with over the last 25 years. I was flooded with memories of walking through secondary schools, decades apart, as a student and as a professional staff member. I was surprised, and concerned, by how familiar and timeless it felt.

Reports about the impact of the series revealed that many young people found the series to be a realistic representation of their lives. For some young people, and adults, the series triggered strong feelings and suicidal thoughts. Some people ended up in hospital following a suicide attempt and, concerningly, reported that watching *13 Reasons Why* contributed to this. Sadly, we now know that some people also died. It was of interest to me that some young people reported that they chose not to watch the series, knowing it may be harmful to them. What willpower it must have taken for young people to disengage from the discussions their friends were having and to know themselves so well that they made the decision to care for themselves first. What struck me most were the reports that the series provided an opportunity for parents and teachers to gain new insights into the lives of teenagers. Research revealed that for many young people and adults caring for them, the series enabled conversations to occur that hadn't been able to take place before. Conversations began to take place about what goes on in the lives of adolescents away from the watchful gaze of adults. These conversations empowered both young people and the adults who care for them to find a bridge to better understand the world of adolescence and most importantly to work together on what can be done to improve the lives of young people. This resonated for me and helped me see that my own life's work had been exactly about that. I've always been curious and had a love of learning. Like most people I have found the area of suicide confronting and interesting — interesting enough to spend three years of my life studying suicidology. The real driver for my interest came from witnessing children and young people struggling with life, experiencing suicidal thoughts and feelings and sometimes acting on them. Their parents and teachers struggled too, not knowing what to do or who to turn to for help. There is probably nothing more confronting as a parent than having your child feeling suicidal or actively hurting themselves. Perhaps the most useful research that came out about the effects of *13 Reasons Why* was the need for both young people and their parents and teachers to have support, to have more resources, and avenues to access information earlier.

I'd had plans already to write a book for parents well before the *13 Reasons Why* series was created. The seeds were sown many years earlier as a community project worker studying psychology in the 1990s and working with groups of parents of teenagers. Later, as a psychologist, continuing to work with parents and in schools, my commitment to finding ways to support parents and their kids continued to strengthen. My doctoral research used a methodology called photovoice (using photos to express ideas and feelings) to look at teenagers' experience of their neighbourhood. The young people's photos I developed at K-Mart (digital photography wasn't commonplace at the time) showed me in no uncertain terms that it was families and home (as well as pets) that really mattered to young people. Again, my commitment to supporting families and the role of parenting was solidified. We can have intentions to do things but we all need a motivator to propel us forward and it was the responses to, and debate about, *13 Reasons Why*, which forced me into action to finally begin work on this book. The gap in information and access to reliable and comprehensive information for parents became clear. While no one book can ever be the answer to complex situations we face, I hope this book gives parents a starting point and a sense of not being alone.

While there's an abundance of books about parenting, experiences of parenting teenagers who are experiencing suicidal thoughts and behaviours aren't well documented. This can be due, perhaps, to some very good reasons, like privacy, guilt and shame. While some of the core messages about parenting stand the test of time, old ideas can be repackaged and branded into what seem to be new ideas. Simplistic recipe-type approaches to parenting can be appealing, but difficult to implement in meaningful ways, particularly at times of crisis. Recipes work best when there are some assumed pre-existing conditions. Parenting always exists within a dynamic between the adults and young people and the broader world with its influences. Each family has its own history, and parents bring to their parenting their own experiences of having been parented, good and bad. All of this sets a backdrop, often without us even realising, which affects the way we view ourselves, our family and our parenting role. Every young person and family is unique and sometimes there are underlying issues that need addressing before simplistic parenting strategies can work. Some books venture into the challenges of parenting and include information about mental health difficulties and what parents should look out for. However, like the topic of suicide in the wider community, there tends to be a silence around parenting experiences when times get really tough and the risk of suicide looms.

In this book, I'll be lifting the lid on what it means to be a parent of a teenager who is struggling with suicidal thoughts and behaviours. I'll draw on my practical experiences of working with parents in community settings over a couple of decades, in schools as a School Psychologist, as a supervisor of psychology interns who often work with people who are suicidal, and as one of the national managers on an Australian national children's mental health initiative. I'll also draw on what I've learned from my long period of study in psychology and recent studies in suicidology. While latest evidence from research and current theories will underpin the book, I'll also reflect on some research and writings from people who have experienced suicidality and the family members who supported them. Mostly though I'll focus on the important role you play as a parent and the practical ideas and strategies that I've seen work for parents.

Perhaps when you pick up this book you've just found out about your teenager's suicide risk and are trying to work out where to start. This will feel overwhelming and frightening. Perhaps you're tempted to not take it seriously, to believe that it can't be real, to think that they're just saying it. I encourage you to take it very seriously and even to see it as an opportunity to understand what is actually going on for your child. Suicidality is complicated and there are many factors that lead to a person becoming suicidal but at the same time it is simple — your child is struggling and needing help. The fact that they have had the courage to trust someone enough to share what's going on for them places you in a position of being able to do something. Taking what they are saying seriously and listening to them needs to be the first step. You might be aware of the need to link your son or daughter into mental health support but it can be hard to know where to begin and what to expect. This can often take time and you and your family will be the people who play the support role throughout and particularly while mental health support is being put in place. Even then, you will continue to be the key support for your child.

On the other hand, perhaps you've heard about youth suicide and want to learn more so that you can be prepared and hopefully prevent the risk of suicide in your family. You might recall your own adolescence and recognise some of the risks or, alternatively, you might have had an easy time in your teenage years so don't feel like you can understand what might lead a young person to become suicidal. You might even have an inkling that something is not quite right. Some readers will have been supporting their teenager through suicidal thoughts and behaviours for some time. You might have tried many things already. No doubt you've learned a lot along the way, but you may still be concerned and wondering if there's anything else you can do. You might be looking for ways to explain what's been happening to family and friends. Clearly, you will have your own reasons for picking up this book. The more at risk your teenager is the more keeping them safe will be your focus. That's the bottom line and everything else only matters if they are safe.

Ultimately, I'm hoping this book will help parents avoid ever becoming one of the families who lose their child. Many teenagers have suicidal thoughts, some attempt suicide and a smaller number die by suicide. We know that we can't entirely control what other people do and you're probably aware already by now that this is certainly the case with teenagers. It is possible though to influence others, to reach out to understand and provide support. While we can do as much as is humanly possible to keep our teenagers safe, the reality is that there is always the possibility that they will still harm themselves. Keeping that in mind, while not allowing it to become your sole focus, will help you make the important decisions about what matters most at any point in time. It will mean you take the risk seriously with a focus on supporting your teenager to stay safe and alive, and ultimately embracing of life.

The purpose of this book

It is probably obvious after reading this far, but I have a couple of key aims in writing this book. They are the same as the aims I had whenever I met with parents or developed resources for parents and educators in my professional roles:

1. to arm parents with knowledge so they can better understand what's going on with their teenager

2. to provide space to reflect on their parenting and to look after themselves

3. to not feel alone; and

4. to know what to do to support their teenagers during difficult times.

Accordingly, the book has two parts: *Part A: Understanding parenting and suicide*, and *Part B: Parenting a teenager who is suicidal*. I've begun with parenting teenagers in general because we need to understand that before we can make sense of why suicidality might be happening and any efforts to respond need to be framed within the context of adolescent development and our relationships. If your teenager begins to struggle with suicidal thoughts or behaviours, you both become caught in an unfamiliar and frightening space. Your teenager may have been in this place for a while already, possibly for some time before you found out. It can help to think about this challenging time as an opportunity to get to know your teenager better so you can, together, gain a deeper understanding of what is going on for him or her. Be ready to learn about yourself too in this process.

It can help you to know that many parents and teenagers have been, and are going, through similar situations and do find ways to come through it. While this book focuses on teenagers, it is important to know that the Australian Bureau of Statistics records deaths by suicide of children aged from 5 years of age. Thankfully deaths by suicide of children and young people are rare but they do happen and many more children and young people have suicidal thoughts and attempts. While focused on adolescence, much of the information here will also apply to younger children and pre-teens and young adults, although there are some obvious differences. I've included information in appendices about this.

A quick note about language

Talking about suicide is important and a critical part of raising awareness and preventing suicide, yet it continues to be problematic. In Australia, we still struggle with how to talk about suicide in the public arena in ways that are safe for everyone. In writing a book about suicide I am aware of the risks that it could create for readers. While it is now agreed that the act of talking about suicide doesn't cause people to become suicidal, we still don't know exactly in what circumstances it might increase the risk of someone becoming suicidal or contribute to their vulnerability to suicide. Australia is leading the world in its guidelines for the media and writers and I'll be following those. For example, I will place messages of self-care throughout, including trigger warnings before specific content about suicide. You can choose to read the sections of the books separately, dipping in and out as it suits you. You might find that some sections are too difficult on some days. You can come in and out of the chapters to take what you need. You can always return to the rest later.

You'll notice that I've used a range of terms to describe the teenager (adolescent, child, young people and teenager — even kids sometimes) throughout the book because at times different words make better sense. Your teenager will always be your child but 'child' doesn't sound right when talking about teenagers. Adolescence is often the term used in research or when talking about the stage of development so at times I've used that term.

The parenting role can take many forms and while I've used the generic term 'parent', I'm intending this to include carers, step parents, extended family members and other adults who take on parenting responsibilities. The more supportive adults a teenager has in their life, and the more cooperative these adults are with each other, the better. What has typically been considered the traditional nuclear family is not the only type of family in Australia. It's abundantly clear that children and young people develop in healthy ways in a range of family configurations so long as there are caring and respectful relationships.

Gender is another consideration I've been aware of while writing this book. Most of my experience has been with mothers who attended groups, attended meetings in schools and came along to individual sessions with me. Similarly, it is often mothers who have participated in research about parenting. It's important to say that fathers also play a critically important role in parenting and can have sole or primary parenting responsibilities for their children. Increasingly, fathers are engaging in help-seeking and want information about ways to support their teenagers and I noticed over the years an increase in fathers attending parenting groups. Research is now looking more at the experiences and needs of fathers, although so far mostly in children's early years. I've therefore aimed to provide a balance between using gender-neutral language and identifying what might be specific gender specific experiences. It's clear we need to hear more male voices. This is a gap that is beyond the scope of this book to attend to.

Increasingly, we're becoming aware of gender and sexuality of children and young people. At times in this book there are gender-specific considerations for children and young people particularly in their identity and understandings of gender and sexuality. Where appropriate, I've named this. This is also a topic that needs much more research and greater discussion, which is also out of scope for this book.

Talking to your teenager about this book

As I've written the book I've had both parents and teenagers in mind. It's impossible to think about parenting without also thinking about the young person. I've also stressed throughout the need for parents to find ways to keep connecting and communicating with their teenagers. Accordingly, there may be sections of the book that you find helpful to check out or share with your teenager. Sometimes it's hard to find the words ourselves, so having a book to read from or refer to can help. If there are things you read that you're not sure about, you can use the book as the platform to have the conversation with your teenager to help explore the topic. You can always say that the book says this and you're not sure whether you agree if that is the case for your family. It can help to let them know that the book is just a starting point or a guide to help you all work out what to do next. Ultimately, we have to work out our own answers.

I'm hoping that if teenagers pick up the book they will find it respectful and useful. Genuine respect occurs when our thoughts and attitudes are respectful, so I've tried to model this throughout. I've tried to raise awareness of the types of experiences that might be happening for your teenager, even though it's impossible to know exactly what is going on in the unique life of each individual. Sometimes I've read books that are dismissive or condescending about adolescents and their experiences (and sometimes not particularly respectful of parents either). I think our teenagers (and parents) deserve better than that so I've tried to present information to build understandings rather than information that promotes simplistic explanations or worse, ridicule or shaming.

When your teenager knows that you are reading a book to seek help through this difficult time, they may respond in various ways. They may or may not let you know that they are pleased that you are trying so hard to help them. I've had young people tell me that they liked the way their parents sought help or told them they didn't have all the answers. They hadn't necessarily told their parents they felt that way. Some parents can feel vulnerable or worry that their teenagers will see this as a weakness and that they are not competent. I'd say that it's much more likely that they will be encouraged and feel more inclined to trust you if you can open up about how you are trying to work out how to get help for the family. Adolescents may feel guilty that they have caused their parents distress. This may lead them to dismiss discussions or push parents away so they can deal with it themselves and stop everyone the worry. Tenacity in parenting is required at those times as you discover different ways to show your teenager you are there for them and want to help them. This book may help them to see that the experiences your family are encountering are not unusual and your family is not the only one experiencing this.

How did you get here?

Although it might seem that this situation has happened overnight, it won't be something that's just arisen from nowhere. We end up in complicated situations because of a complex mix of things that come together at a point in time. This is especially the case for people who are suicidal and their families. While it's often tempting to look for simple explanations to help us make sense of our world, this is not likely to be the case here. There might have been a recent trigger that has set off this current situation and it might look like that's the sole reason for your teenager's response. In fact, there's probably been a whole of smaller things building up along the way. Some of these are difficult to notice at the time, some of them can't be changed and some of them only begin to make sense as we get the chance to look back on them later. Deciding to read this book might be an important step in your journey to understanding and improving the current situation with your teenager.

Understanding parenting and suicide

The storm has set in. Dark clouds cluster on the horizon, and the sky feels electric with change. Nothing feels the same, and yet you can't quite pinpoint what's different. Your child looks the same. Your surroundings appear the same. And yet the inner compass that guides all your parenting decisions feel like it's spinning out of control.

(Douglas, 2017, p. 28)

This is the way that Ann Douglas begins her book about parenting during difficult times, *Parenting Through the Storm*. She goes on to describe herself as feeling helpless and overwhelmed, a totally incompetent parent. She worried about what would happen to each of her kids. While she knew she had to do something, she didn't know what that was.

Parenting brings a heap of emotions and challenges. Some of those challenges can be reasonably expected while others are hard to be prepared for. Each child in the family is different and while we believe we are parenting in the same way for all of them, the family unit is constantly changing just as we, as individuals, are also changing all the time. We sometimes unknowingly carry expectations from an older child to our expectations for a younger child for example. We also continue to learn about parenting as the years pass. This means that our parenting can't be the same for each child, although there are likely to be core values and beliefs that don't change too much, whether we are aware or not. Often these come from our own family of origin.

Parenting occurs within the vacuum of everyday life, increasingly busy times where we all have our own lives and come together as a family at different points during the day. Noticing what's going on for each other can be difficult when we are busy with our own life matters. Parenting experiences can shift as children reach adolescence and the line between what is normal, healthy behaviour and development in teenagers and what might be signs of impending trouble is not always clear. Sometimes we can't tell until afterwards that something was tipping onto the side of problematic. Hindsight has a way of helping us see things more clearly.

Suicide is a confronting topic and as a parent may represent our greatest fear for our family. When we are faced with difficult topics it's common for us to want to put our heads in the sand and not think about it. There's been a lot of confusion too about whether talking about suicide can be harmful with concerns that it might give someone the idea. This has now been largely discredited and in fact the opposite is now considered to be the case — that not talking about suicide can be harmful. Knowing how to talk about suicide and reaching a point of readiness to do this might need us to do some thinking about it for ourselves and learning more about it so we are able to have honest conversations with our kids, be open and prepared for what they might tell us and, importantly, know what to do if they share their experiences of suicidality. As with a lot of areas of parenting teenagers, being prepared for conversations about difficult topics will help us to be more confident, able to be there for our kids and help them find ways to get through challenging times.

Learning about suicide means facing the fact that there is a risk that this may happen. It can be challenging and I encourage you to think about how you will care for yourself while reading these chapters. Perhaps read them in short bursts, read it them with someone or have someone to talk to at the time. Be ready for a range of emotions and don't be afraid of those emotions. Let them tell you something about yourself and what you are worried about. Remember that there is a list of help lines in the Introduction that you can use if you are finding yourself distressed.

Ultimately, our teenager is their own unique individual. While we can look at typical experiences of adolescence your teenager will bring their own personality and life experiences. Part of the role of parents is to help them find and appreciate that uniqueness and use it to propel themselves forward in ways that are life-embracing.

Chapter 1

Being a parent of a teenager

Parenting experiences

For centuries, parents have been confronted with the period of time known as adolescence — the developmental period between childhood and adulthood. While in the past this period typically fell between the ages of 13 and 17 years, in recent decades this age range has spread, with adolescence now stretching from 10 to 25 years (or even older). The reasons for this are varied, perhaps (if I'm cynical) partly driven in the western world by marketing efforts related to the adolescent age group, but beyond economic impacts there are also biological and social factors. Children in the western world experience puberty at a younger age than in the past. This combines with social and economic factors where they are entering into adulthood and independence from parents later as they stay at school longer and economic pressures related to becoming independent increase. We also now know more about the way the adolescent brain continues to develop into adulthood. This can help us understand some of the behaviours of young people and why our expectations are sometimes not met. As it is new, it's good to remember that we are still learning about this and caution is therefore warranted. Anything that is understood from a purely neuroscientific perspective is likely to miss the significant social and cultural factors that are such an important part of human development.

As people develop from childhood into adolescence and then to adulthood, they are confronted by the same challenges generations before them have faced — the search for identity; coping with physical, emotional and social changes that occur throughout childhood and peak during adolescence; finding ways to participate meaningfully in their community and the world; and to gradually renegotiate relationships with the adults around them, particularly those people closest to them, like family. Research about the needs of young people finds that relationships and strong attachments to both family and peers are critically important to their development, mental health and quality of life. Young people themselves often talk about their interest in being supported by family members while at the same time spending time and having fun with their peers — and at times pushing their parents away. It's a difficult space to navigate and it's easy for communication to break down, perhaps oscillating between extremes of withdrawal or silence to intense conflict.

Adolescence has been described variously as a time of conflict and stress, of disappointment and grief, but also of tremendous pride and relief. The role of parents during this time of rapid change has been challenged and questioned not only by young people themselves but also by society more broadly. Schools, for example, can reach out to parents, while at the same time promoting the independence and self-reliance they expect young people to develop. Young people get mixed messages about their independence; on one hand they are expected to be independent and responsible yet on the other they are still dependent on adults. Parents can sometimes feel blamed when things go wrong for young people. Accordingly, their role is increasingly unclear. Parents can experience this as a lack of power or influence. This means that their role can be minimised, leaving them and their young people disconnected, at the very time when connection is so critical.

Historically, stress and conflict have been considered features of this period but increasingly, contemporary research on adolescence within western societies suggests that conflict between parents and teenagers may not occur as much as once thought. Of course, adolescents and their families are not all the same. Some will experience more struggles than others, the degree of struggle often depending upon the kind of stressors they experience and the level of support available to them. All of this raises many questions for parents and young people which are not yet answered and there's good reason for parents to feel uncertain about how well they're doing in their parenting role.

Rapidly changing technologies mean that young people are now able to access information and communicate with each other in ways that were not possible for their parents and grandparents. This can lead to new knowledge, access to information not previously available and new jobs in the information technology arena. Just what impact does all of this have on their day to day lives, their ongoing development and the relationships they have with the most significant people in their lives, such as their family? It's early days and it's hard to know but it's fair to say that while there are many positives, there are also some worrying signs that we're best not to ignore. Given the conflicting research, it's clear that we are yet to fully understand and integrate these new ways of communicating. Adults still seem to express ambivalence about technology, while for young people it is core to their existence. We are often focused on the negatives or what we think might be negatives (and like everything there are risks and concerns) but in doing that we might be missing opportunities. By rethinking our attitudes to technology and keeping up with it, we might be able to find ways to use it to improve our lives and build closer relationships with each other.

Attachment

As a Community Psychologist, I have a particular interest in the relationships we have with each other — in families, workplaces and communities. The whole idea of community is based on the value of relationships and opportunities to gain meaning in our lives through our social networks and interactions. We form relationships with people for different reasons. Sometimes we have interests and find ourselves attracted to people who share those. We might describe this as finding 'our people' or 'our tribe'. It's pleasant to be with people who share our interests or values. Sometimes we connect with people who meet other needs at a point in time. Relationships are complex and dynamic, and home is the first place where relationship skills are developed and tested out.

When we become parents we typically draw on our early experiences as children to form attachment or a bond with our own children. While it can sound simple to bond with a baby, this experience is not always as easy as it seems. If we are experiencing physical or mental health difficulties or the baby is restless or unwell, the bonding experience may take longer than expected or we may need support. While we've understood the importance of developing secure attachments in childhood for some time, it's only been in recent years that we have begun to really appreciate how important attachments are across the entire lifespan. How we form our very early relationships with our primary caregivers in many ways sets the blueprint for future abilities to form strong relationships. Those first few years are critical to our development but it by no means ends there. Our childhood friendships are the first place outside of the family for us to test out our relationship skills. During adolescence this is tested further as we learn to form more intense and different types of relationships, including romantic relationships.

Relationships are important throughout our lives. Developing healthy relationships with others requires us to have an established sense of ourselves. We need to be able to place our trust in others. We learn about this from our childhood. You may have heard about secure and insecure attachment. These ideas are based on the work of John Bowlby and Mary Ainsworth who argued that early attachment figures (primary caregiver, usually considered to be the mother) acted as a secure base for children to explore the world. This early attachment relationship is understood, in attachment theory, to set the scene for all future social relationships. During the first year of life, a critical developmental need is the formation of an attachment bond between an infant and his mother. The infant relies on the mother to respond to his or her 'attachment behaviours', communicated through crying or crawling, in order to be close (or have what they called 'proximity') to the attachment figure. If the attachment figure responds quickly and with sensitivity, and the child can achieve proximity when distressed, the child feels safe and protected. If the mother or caregiver fails to respond in this manner, the infant may turn to other, less direct strategies that fulfill the goal of proximity. In some cases, the child may not achieve proximity at all due to the caregiver's inability to provide care. In such a case the child is left unprotected. Over time, the infant develops an 'internal working model' based on these interactions with their caregiver. This internal working model is essentially a set of rules that the child uses to predict future behaviour and interactions involved in social relationships. Researchers have used attachment theory to understand how relationships develop or change over the course of childhood, adolescence and into adulthood.

While we can accept that the first years of life are important, we also know that infants are highly resilient and adaptive and even when there are challenges in the quality of parenting care they receive they may not be irreparably damaged. The ability of humans to seek out connection and self-repair can ensure that people can develop healthy relationships even if their early childhood years were not ideal in terms of attachment figures. Parents and infants are constantly moving in and out of 'synch' with each other. Babies can soothe themselves when mismatches occur, and also break contact when overstimulated. It can be useful to think about the parent-adolescent relationship in terms of this ability to be in 'synch' with each other — what I often think about as a dance where each person responds to the other, staying close by and adjusting as necessary.

As our children develop, the attachment process continues, and the cycle of attachment from our own childhood continues, with us gradually learning to let go as children grow. Bowlby and Ainsworth's work is important because it taught us that when children are securely attached they are more able to leave us, returning every now and again for reassurance. Some children have personalities or experiences that affect this, with some children being more cautious and requiring reassurance. Over the years of childhood and adolescence we need to find ways to continue the attachment so that it feels like a strong bond, while at the same time enabling the child to develop into their own person with the confidence to make their own decisions, develop their own friendships and over time become independent.

Parenting styles

Parenting styles relate to the broad patterns of childrearing practices, values and behaviours. Parenting styles are closely related to the relationship we develop with our children, the influence we can have over our teenager, the development of the teenager and a range of outcomes for the teenager. The most famous work that influenced Western approaches to parenting styles was undertaken by Baumrind during the 1960s and still has relevance today, although we are perhaps more open now to the idea that parents use more than one style, depending upon the circumstances. Baumrind was interested in the way that parenting styles affected teenagers' social development. She described three main parenting styles:

- *Authoritative (clear, high expectations with emotional support and recognition of the child's autonomy)*. Parents using this style listen to children, explain and discuss options, allow children to be independent and learn for themselves, give responsibilities suitable for the child's age and ability rather than over-protecting them or doing too much for them, understand children's temperament and stage of development, and respond to situations based on the needs of the child rather than being over-run by their own emotions. Parents are warm and loving and provide clear guidance and support. They are supported to do well at school and encouraged to try their best and achieve. Children are more likely to be emotionally mature, have better social skills, self-confidence and wellbeing. It is abundantly clear through many research studies that authoritative parenting works best for children and this has been shown recently in relation to suicidal behaviour of teenagers. Recent research found that telling children parents are proud of them, that they did a good job and helping them with homework have been found to be particularly important in protecting teenagers against suicide, particularly during early adolescence.

- *Authoritarian (parent tries to shape, control and evaluate the behaviour and attitudes of the child in accordance with a set standard of conduct)*. Parents using this style tell children what to do and expect them to obey and may not give reasons. They aim for obedience rather than helping children learn what is expected. They can be controlling, lack warmth and may be overly strict and harsh, may have limited understanding of children's development and expect them to do things they are not yet able to. Parents can react based on their own mood rather than the situation. Parents may have high expectations but not provide the necessary support to help children do well. Children growing up with this parenting style may be quite obedient and know the rules but may have lower self-worth and can become defiant and aggressive. They may depend on others to make decisions and be less likely to take on responsibilities or solve problems.

- *Permissive (nonpunitive, accepting and affirmative manner towards the child's impulses, desires and actions).* Parents using this style are warm, loving and responsive but provide very little or no discipline or guidance. They may give in to children's demands too often, tending not to set firm limits. They can be inconsistent and don't follow through on consequences and may allow children's behaviour to negatively affect others. Children may grow up feeling loved but insecure due to the lack of boundaries. They don't learn appropriate behaviour or how to be responsible. They may lack self-discipline, have poor social skills and be too self-involved.

As you read through these descriptions, you may be thinking about your own experiences — perhaps as a child growing up in your family of origin, and perhaps as the parenting style you use in your own family now. Throughout this book the approaches and strategies will be based on an authoritative parenting style as this is the parenting style consistently shown to have the best outcomes.

Being a 'good enough' parent

There's perhaps been no other time in history when parenting has been under so much scrutiny. It seems that the more access we have to information, the more we question ourselves and the more others share their opinions about how they think parenting should happen. We can also be exposed to a whole range of information, some of it very helpful, and some of it very unhelpful. At the very least, it can feel overwhelming to be inundated with so much information. This occurs because of the importance we place on parenting. We know it's important and we want to do it well. We've also had our own experience of being parented and there may be some aspects of that experience that we want to use and some other aspects that we wouldn't want to do or that no longer fit as times have changed.

One of the most useful ideas about parenting that I've ever come across is the idea of 'good enough' parenting. This idea originally came from a paediatrician and psychoanalyst, Donald Winnicott. He worked as a paediatrician at the Paddington Green Hospital in London and came into contact with many mothers and their babies. Through this day to day experience of interacting with families, he came to believe that the way to be a 'good mother' (parent) is to be a 'good enough mother' (parent) (Winnicott,

1987). In 1953 he recognised the need for children to realise that a mother is not good or bad, but is a separate and independent entity. He said that the good-enough mother starts off with an almost complete adaptation to her infant's needs, and as time proceeds, she adapts less and less completely, gradually, according to the infant's growing ability to deal with her failure. It is this failure to adapt to every need of the child that helps them adapt to external realities.

While Winnicott encouraged parents to be realistic about their role, there has been considerable debate since then about exactly what is necessary to meet children's needs. Dr Andrew Wake, an Australian child and adolescent psychiatrist, in a book titled *The 'Good Enough' Parent*, recognises the way in which parenting can lead to self-doubt in parents. He reflects on the parents he works with who confront him with concerns like 'Am I doing the right thing?', 'Is it my fault that he's like this?' and 'Please tell me what to do'. His book begins with explaining the importance of attachment and safety as well as current thinking about brain development. He then outlines various approaches to parenting — a playful approach, a supportive approach, a repairing approach, an experienced approach and a co-operative approach (Wake, 2012). While the examples in the book refer to younger children, it's useful for us to reflect on these various approaches when parenting a teenager. By the time our children are teenagers we may have become stuck in a particular approach. This may or may not be helpful. It may feel comfortable, safe, and normal to us. Perhaps the more concerned we become the more serious and stuck we become. The idea of being playful with teenagers might sound ridiculous but there may be a place to consider this. Shifting our way of relating to another person might be what's needed to break through some of the barriers in communicating that will enable new ways to relate to each other. The very nature of our changing relationship during the teenage years means that we need to be alert to our needs as well as the teenager's. There may be upsets and tensions that come with these changes.

Wake then outlines the basics of what it means to be a good enough parent:

- Provide enough safety
- Provide for their basic needs
- Provide enough unity

- Provide enough affectionate care

- Provide enough boundaries.

Wakes' final chapter is particularly relevant to parents of teenagers. It's all about reflecting more and reacting less. He describes reacting as taking on their emotion, responding as leaving the emotion with them and reflecting as giving the emotion back to them. He describes this process as requiring us to be in tune with our children, to be with them as they are without trying to control them, seeing them as separate to ourselves rather than as an extension of ourselves and to interact with them as they are rather than as we wish them to be (Wake, 2012). We need to be aware of our own feelings, understanding and restraining them if necessary. He acknowledges that it is these emotions that make parenting so tricky. Ideally, we have learned all of this when our children are younger and we've been practising this through-out their lives so by the time they're teenagers we are building on this foun-dation. In reality though for many parents this isn't the approach they've taken. This is particularly the case if their teenager has been a pretty easy-going child and it's only as a teenager that the parent has begun to question their parenting skills. The good news is that it's never too late to learn new ways of parenting and finding ways to open up communication. It neces-sarily begins with our own self-awareness of our emotions and finding ways to manage those. This in turn helps us to not only deal with situations with better managed emotions but also sets the scene for modelling for our teenagers about how to communicate in helpful and respectful ways. It can help to know that you don't have to do this perfectly — in fact as we've read being good enough is enough but that includes being ready to apologise and repair damage that may be caused if we said or did things that were hurtful. Learning about this can take time and for many parents attending a parent-ing group or seeing a health professional can be useful to develop and practice these new skills. Appendix C includes a list of parenting programs that are consistent with this approach.

Reflection: The meaning of parenting to you

- How would you describe your experience as a parent? Is there one word that fits?

- Is there a parenting style that stands out as the style you tend to use in your parenting at the moment?

- What does the role of parent look like for you at the moment? Has this always been the case or has it changed over time?

- What other roles in your life do you share with your parenting role?

- What influence does your background have on your views and experience of parenting? Consider your cultural background, your religious views, your family history.

- Who shares the responsibilities of parenting with you? What does that look like?

- How do you show your teenager love?

- What word would you use to describe your relationship with your teenager? Is there an image or song that comes to mind?

- How do you provide routines, rituals and guidance to help them feel safe and secure?

- How do you help teenagers understand their behaviours?

- What are your three key goals as a parent right now?

- How have these goals changed over time? In the last year? In the last five years? What has triggered these changes?

- What are your three current strengths as a parent? Have these changed over time?

- What areas of your parenting would you like to strengthen?

- How can you strengthen these areas? Who or what can help?

Chapter 2

Teenage development

One of the most obvious signs of adolescence is the significant physical changes that are characteristic of the developmental stage. We now know that well before the physical changes become visible to others, these changes have been enabled through a process of hormones being triggered. Both visible and hidden changes can affect all aspects of the young person's body and mind: their sense of who they are, their place in the family and society, their assumptions about the world around them, their capacity to do things (and perceptions about what they can do) and their relationships with family members, peers and teachers. It can begin what may well become a lifelong questioning, shaped variously by relationships with others across the course of the lifespan. The 'work' of adolescence to test boundaries and explore new things can lay the path for the development of their future selves of adventure and purpose.

It is now recognised that the changes associated with adolescence are tending to occur much earlier than in the past. Researchers have measured puberty since the 1940s when key aspects of adolescent development, including socio-emotional, cognitive and behavioural impacts, began to be observed and studied. During the 1990s studies began to report puberty beginning considerably earlier than in previous decades, as early as 6 or 7 years age in girls based on breast development although age at menarche (first menstruation period) was older. Factors such as nutrition and social class have been cited as factors responsible for this change however there is still uncertainty about causes. Knowing about this is important because the early timing of puberty has found to be related to negative psychological (e.g. depression) and behavioural (e.g. risky behaviours, acting out) outcomes, although there is considerable variability also noted in research. Impacts of puberty can relate directly due to the brain changes which arise during that time and indirectly through the responses of parents and peers who observe the pubertal changes and behave differently towards them (e.g. increase their expectations). Early puberty, technically known as premature adrenarche, is currently defined as occurring in girls 8 years or younger and in boys aged 9 years or younger. Puberty is no longer seen as a discrete or one-off event but rather as a process involving a series of changes in different parts of the body which follow their own pathway in a complicated way with each aspect of pubertal development having its own unique meaning.

Brain development and neuroscience

The last two decades have seen new understandings about the human brain, particularly during early childhood, childhood and adolescence. We now accept that the human brain continues to develop well into our mid-20s (taking longer to fully develop in males than females) with changes occurring at peak periods such as puberty. We also accept that the areas of the brain that are most used are the areas that are likely to be strengthened, with pruning of underutilised areas. This is a very simplistic explanation of the complexities of the brain and there is still much we are continuing to learn about the abilities and limitations of the adolescent brain, particularly as development and growth occurs within the context of technology use. There is also a tension that comes with these discussions: if we don't expect much of our teenagers because we believe their brain is still developing we don't provide them with the opportunity to develop that comes from having expectations; on the other hand if we are too critical of them or don't understand the limitations or weaknesses of the adolescent brain we may be expecting too much of them which is unfair and unhelpful to our relationship.

Brain development during adolescence is important to know about because it impacts the way young people remember, think, reason, focus attention, make decisions and relate to others. During adolescence (typically between 12 and 24 years) there is a burst of growth and maturation that hasn't taken place before. According to Dr Dan Siegel, an American Psychiatrist, these brain changes during the early teen years set up four qualities of adolescent minds, each with its own positives and negatives (see Table 2.1).

Search for identity and meaning

This search for identity and meaning during adolescence has long been recognised as a key feature of this period of the human lifespan. Over 40 years ago, Erik Erikson, a German-American developmental psychologist and psychoanalyst had this to say about adolescent development:

> [Y]oung people, beset with the physiological revolution of their genital maturation and the uncertainty of the adult roles ahead, seem much concerned with faddish attempts at establishing an adolescent subculture with what looks like a final rather than a transitory, or, in fact, initial identity formation' (Erikson, 1968, p. 128).

He continues with a description of how this can play out to the observer:

> [t]hey are sometimes morbidly, often curiously, preoccupied with what they appear to be in the eyes of others as compared with what they feel they are, and with the question of how to connect the roles and skills cultivated earlier with the ideal prototypes of the day. In their search for a new sense of continuity and sameness, which must now include sexual maturity, some adolescents have to come to grips again with crises of earlier years before they can install lasting idols and ideals as guardians of a final identity. They need, above all, a moratorium for the integration of the identity elements ascribed in the foregoing to the childhood stages: only that now a larger unit, vague in its outline and yet immediate in its demands, replaces the childhood milieu — 'society'. A review of these elements is also a list of adolescent problems. (Erikson, 1968, p. 128)

It can be comforting as a parent to read this and see its relevance decades later. This search for meaning and sense making of past and present life experiences has been described by Erikson as 'locomotion', general being 'on the go', 'running around' or 'shiftless Wanderschaft'. He also recognised

Table 2.1 Four qualities of adolescent minds

Brain change	Effects	Positive	Negative
1. Novelty seeking	Emerges from an increased drive for rewards in the circuits of the adolescent brain that creates the inner motivation to try something new and feel life more fully, creating more engagement in life.	Being open to change and living passionately develop into a fascination for life and a drive to design new ways of doing things and living with a sense of adventure.	Sensation seeking and risk taking that overemphasise the thrill and downplay the risk resulting in dangerous behaviours and injury. Impulsivity can make an idea turn into an action with a pause to reflect on the consequences.
2. Social engagement	Enhances peer connectedness and creates new friendships.	The drive for social connection leads to the creation of supportive relationships that are the research-proven best predictors of wellbeing, longevity, and happiness throughout the life span.	Teens isolated from adults and surrounded only by other teenagers can have increased risk behaviour, and the total of adults and adult knowledge and reasoning increases those risks.
3. Increased emotional intensity	Gives an enhanced vitality to life.	Life lived with emotional intensity can be filled with energy and a sense of vital drive that give an exuberance and zest for being alive on the planet.	Intense emotion may rule the day, leading to impulsivity, moodiness and extreme, sometimes, unhelpful reactivity.
4. Creative exploration with an expanded sense of consciousness	An adolescent's new conceptual thinking and abstract reasoning allow questioning of the status quo, approaching problems with 'out of the box' strategies, the creation of new ideas, and the emergence of innovation.	If the mind can hold on to thinking and imagining and perceiving the world in new ways within consciousness, of creatively exploring the spectrum of experiences that are possible, the sense of being in a rut that can sometimes pervade adult life can be minimised and instead an experience of the 'ordinary being extraordinary' can be cultivated.	Searching for the meaning of life during the teen years can lead to a crisis of identity, vulnerability to peer pressure and a lack of direction and purpose.

Note: Adapted from Siegel, D. (2013). Brainstorm: The Power and Purpose of the Teenage Brain.

that this energy can play out in participation in movements of the day, through campaigns or protests involving ideology (such as climate change rallies). He stated that society even offered ritualistic opportunities for this to occur through demonstrations, dance, riots and parades, in efforts to harness the energy of young people. If society does not enable these opportunities, he asserts that young people will find their own ways to do this, sometimes through pranks, foolishness or delinquency. He summarised this search for meaning as part of the overall identity development when he stated, 'In no other stage of the life cycle, then, are the promise of finding oneself and the threat of losing oneself so closely allied' (Erikson, 1968, p. 244).

Although identity development can be an ongoing life journey for all of us as we search to find our own unique being, adolescence is the period when this search can be intense and may dominate the life of the adolescent. It is a core developmental task for them — in some ways the work of adolescence. There are many aspects to personal identity which occurs through a complex interplay of influences:

- Popular culture, including lifestyle options, and consumerism and engagement with technology

- Distinctive cultural and/or religious heritage

- National identification, which takes into account the overall social and political context

- Personal needs, interests, and ambitions.

- Family and friendship groups

Friendships are included with family as they, like family, are significant influences on teenagers. All these influences come together to impact on teenagers, both supporting the development of an identity or leading to issues with identity as the various influences interact with each other. These influences are useful to consider because they highlight the various interactions which occur in the life of a young person at any point in time but also acknowledge the factors which have been part of the person's life, perhaps without them realising it. The factors not only impact on the young person's life in the present but can also affect the young person's future hopes and expectations.

This can help us understand what might be called 'moral identity' where the young person's beliefs, motives and behaviours combine with their self-knowledge. This awareness continues to develop as the young person increases understandings through experiences. While the young person's personal identity is unique and defined through this process it also involves a lifelong process of continual reflection and change. When those factors come together, personal identity develops and includes the following:

- Gender and sexual identity

- Family identification — the young person may identify with a family or group of families

- Belonging to a group or multiple groups — the young person may join various groups for activities but also have a group-related sub-identity

- Religion or spirituality — extent to which the young person draws on religious traditions to describe and live out their identity

- Values, beliefs, ethical code and commitments that give direction to life and interactions with others (sometimes referred to as morals)

- Retail — effects of consumer goods and the media orchestrated images that go with them

- Cultural — identification with particular cultural groups and styles in their lives

- Historical — the impact of historical events which impact on the young person

- Work and study — the effect of schooling/training and employment (or lack of) on the individual's sense of self

- Psychological — the young person's understanding of themselves, their needs, feelings, interests, attitudes, values and patterns of behaviour. This could include ideals, passions and commitments.

Exploring ways of being to establish an identity or being uncertain about who we are can lead to experimentation. Being accepted by a social group can provide an identity haven but can also require a high level of conformity in appearance, interests, activities, in-language, music and places to spend time. This involves a dynamic where young people can be influenced by the group but also influence the group and make some choices about whether to stay as a member of the group or not, depending upon whether their needs are being met.

One of the features of adolescence that can be concerning to the adults around them is risk taking behaviours, an apparent fearlessness or lack of regard for danger. Again Erikson had something to say about this:

> The evidence in young lives of the search for something and somebody to be true to can be seen in a variety of pursuits more or less sanctioned by society... this search is often misunderstood, and often it is only dimly perceived by the individual himself, because youth, always set to grasp both diversity in principle and principle in diversity, must often test extremes before settling on a considered course. These extremes, particularly in times of ideological confusion and widespread marginality of identity, may include not only rebellious but also deviant, delinquent, and self-destructive tendencies. (1968, p. 235)

The role of others, or the community, assists in the young person defining themselves, as like or not like others. It's no surprise then that today's young people find technology attractive, providing interactive ways to communicate, interesting ways to spend their time and engaging ways to learn and play with the world around them. They have grown up with technology surrounding them and being a constant part of their lives. This generation has been referred to as digital natives (compared to previous generations who are digital immigrants). Digital natives often interact with multiple technologies at one time, use technology in all facets of their lives and see it as part of their day to day lives. As a core part of their existence, technology can meet many of their needs: as an information source, communication device and an opportunity to continue to find new ways to do things. Its rapid development brings a need to keep up to date with the latest device or piece of equipment and this even adds to the excitement and energy that technology brings. For young people unable to physically participate in activities in the real world community (due to illness or disability), access provided through social networking sites can keep them in touch with what is going on around them and help them to feel part of the broader social world which exists — tapping into an aspect of their development which is key to their stage of development. They are able to expand their social world through participating in online groups, sharing interests and networking in ways that would not always be possible in a physical space. They can share their ideas and gain feedback on these ideas within a matter of minutes from their virtual community, not just their immediate geographical area.

Importance of friends and belonging

As part of adolescent development, young people start to become more interested in the world outside of the family. You may recall this yourself as a teenager where you experienced a shift in how you saw your family. During my early adolescence we lived in a small beachside town and one of our family rituals on warm, summer nights was to buy an ice-cream and drive around the beaches, perhaps pausing at one of the beaches to watch the waves crashing across the rocks. We'd witness the return of the mutton birds to their nests, greeting their babies waiting anxiously for their day's food supply. I recall feeling so embarrassed driving around the town with my family that I would duck down in the back seat as we drove around the town. Being seen by my friends was a very real concern and I was mortified at the thought. This felt like an innate pull towards prioritising my friends over my family. I now return to that country town for holidays (and strangely I still do that drive around the beaches). As I do this, I'm reminded of how I felt as a teenager, reflecting on how influential that time is in our development. It reinforces to me that we are instinctively social beings and fitting in is a critical part of our lives.

While children certainly value and enjoy friendships, there is a definite shift during adolescence where this need to fit in and belong to the peer group becomes much more important and related to who we are. It's not simply how we spend our time or have fun. While it is part of breaking away from parents towards independence, it can be confusing when teenagers are still so connected to their parents, even if it's not so obvious in a public sense. As we learn more about attachment and the importance of relation-ships across the lifespan we can place this adolescent period in context and appreciate its value in helping our kids form attachments to others.

With the development of these new relationships can come fears for parents about the kinds of friendships our kids are making. We may have strong preferences and expectations about the kinds of kids they should spend time with. We may have received messages during our own adoles-cence about being judged by the 'company we keep'. It's useful to bear in mind that we all seek out people who we can relate to. Perhaps they are people like us or people we admire. Sometimes we can be attracted to people who are different to us because we are curious or want to find out what it would be like to be more like them. Bear in mind also that adolescents are undergoing their own search for who they are, so it's natural that they want to try out new ways of acting or of seeing the world in a different way. Experimenting with being with other young people who are the same or different to them can be an important and healthy part of this.

There might be times when you are genuinely concerned about your teenager's choice of friends, particularly if you are noticing changes in attitudes and behaviours that relate to risk or trouble. Again it can be helpful to think about your own experiences of testing this out as an adolescent. Even though I was very compliant as a child and adolescent, I do recall getting in trouble once during my secondary school days. It was for talking and laughing with my friend, the one friend from school I have continued to keep in touch with as an adult. She taught me other ways to be at school and the experience of being sent out of the classroom gave me insight into what it was like to behave in a different way. I didn't particularly like it, so I learned from the experience to be more cautious in future (I didn't stop talking but I was certainly more aware of doing it in ways where I didn't get caught). I especially didn't like the very serious conversation with my mum after parent-teacher interviews where the teacher raised concerns that I was being negatively influenced. Part of my development then was to learn to manage the friendship (which I valued) and testing out new ways of being without losing my way or stressing out my parents too much. Given that I was often a passive student it was actually really important for me to test out a new way to be, to know that I could behave differently if I chose but learning that there would be consequences for my behaviour, particularly in those days when teachers talked and the students listened and spoke when asked to.

When young people don't feel connected to friends they risk experiencing loneliness. Studies around the world, particularly the United Kingdom, are now finding that suicide risk can be related to loneliness. Making and keeping friends requires a range of social and emotional skills and it will be helpful for young people if parents can understand the importance of friendships and help young people navigate their social world so that they are connected and emotionally and physically safe within their social environments, both virtual and real world.

Where do parents fit in?

With the significant changes that occur for adolescents during puberty and throughout the adolescent period, it's clear that the role of parents is likely to be less clear than when children were younger. The tension between dependence and independence provides one way to explain some of the features that characterise the parent-adolescent relationship. As the young person moves through the adolescent period seeking new freedoms and more control over his or her life, they value being able to test things out, do things differently to the way their families have done them and to be given space to make at least some of their own decisions. At the same time, parents become concerned about their safety and respect for self and others. There may also be hopes and expectations that parents have held for many years about their children as adolescents and young adults which may or may not be realised. There may similarly be different ideas between young people and their parents about these expectations and plans. There may be a lack of consensus about the priority to be given to the here and now and planning for the future. What this looks like may appear different to each party and in fact parents' concern and care can be easily interpreted by adolescents as attempts to control their lives, to continue to treat them like children rather than the emerging adults they see themselves as.

This occurs within a context in which the young person also values and needs the support the family provides, feels nurtured by the presence of the family and gains a sense of trust and attachment which enables them to venture into the world outside of the family home. This is a great paradox which can confuse parents and adolescents alike — the young person pushing the parent away while still needing them to be close. It's easy in such a situation for misunderstandings to occur and for minor conflicts to become bigger than they need to be. Add to this the mix of the temperaments of the young person and each parent or caregiver, roles within the family, external pressures and expectations and past patterns of communicating and you could well have a recipe for confusion and distress. Knowing about these contradictions can be helpful for the parent and adolescent in aiming to better understand each other and finding ways to meet needs without infringing on what is most important to each other.

Increasingly for the parent during the adolescent years their role can feel irrelevant and be dismissed despite the ongoing dependence that the young person has on the parent and family unit. This can diminish the sense of influence and value the parent feels in their role and lead to a lack of confidence as they struggle to find ways to enable them to be there for the young person in a useful and age-appropriate manner. Parents may find that what may have been useful for one child in the family may prove to be unwanted and unhelpful for another child. What one child needed or valued may not be the same for others and this adds more confusion to the overall parenting role and sense of efficacy or self-confidence needed for parents to parent well. For parents going through the adolescent period with their teenager for the first time their role can be confusing and knowing where, when and how to place boundaries can be very difficult. Depending on the temperament and interests of the young person, the efforts of the parent may be encouraged or dismissed. Parents can feel like they are walking a tight rope as they navigate this new space together — leaning too far to one side can lead to the young person being pushed away, leaning to the other extreme and being too protective of the young person can mean they push the boundaries further. Not being there when the young person needs them can prove to be disappointing and further invalidating of the role. This is not an easy space to navigate.

Despite the inconsistencies of this experience, research consistently highlights the important role that parents and other family members play in the lives of young people. In surveys conducted each year by Mission Australia (2018), young people regularly identify family relationships as significant along with friendships. In the 2018 research 28,286 young people aged between 15 and 19 years were surveyed. They were asked how much they value family relationships and 83.7% of respondents stated that they valued these highly (53% reporting that they were extremely important). Friendships were seen similarly, with over eight in ten young people responding that they highly valued these. When asked about issues of personal concern to them, families were also included. The young people surveyed were asked about sources of support for issues that were important in their lives. Again families were seen as significant although their friends were also important (76.1% said parents and/or guardians, 60.1% said relative/family friend and 84.5% said friends).

Around half of the young people surveyed indicated that they would go to a general practitioner (GP) or health professional (53.8%), their brother or sister (53.3%) or the internet (49.4%) for help with important issues in their lives. Nearly four in ten would turn to a teacher (37.7%) as a source of help with important issues in their lives. These statistics reveal that although family is important to young people, the parent is not the all-encompassing source of support they may have been when their children were younger, they do complement the support young people receive from others, particularly peers and teachers.

The role of families in the lives of adolescents was also found to be important in the research undertaken by myself for my Doctorate in Community Psychology. It began by looking at the role of neighbourhood and communities in the lives of young people. Community psychologists are interested in the ways that people fit within their environments and ideas of what community is and how it supports people. I was interested in how young people began to engage in their community. I gave a group of young people a disposable camera and asked them to take photos that showed me how they spend their time. I did receive some photos of community activities, but overwhelmingly, film after film I developed showed images of family life. Bedrooms, kitchens with toast, bathrooms with hair products, pets (lots of pets!) and family members. Stories came through about the role of family members in their lives. In fact it overshadowed the neighbourhood so much I had to shift my focus and write the thesis about the importance of family in the lives of young people. As a qualitative researcher with an exploratory topic I was able to do this. At the time I was grateful that I used the cameras to give the young people a real voice. The alternative (which I had tried but it hadn't worked well) was to ask them to complete a questionnaire based on what I thought was important. If I had stuck with that approach, I would have been so far off the mark that it would have been embarrassing and not portrayed the reality of young people's lives. Through this study I was able to identify the following roles that families play in the lives of young people:

1. *Identity.* As parents remain the constant in the lives of adolescents, they know them well and assist in the development of their identity.

This could provide a grounding role during times of change.

2. *Connection.* Contact with extended family members who live overseas was reported as were family rituals such as get-togethers. These seemed to be associated with enjoyment and fun and storytelling that appeared to help consolidate the adolescent's place within the family.

3. *Shared characteristics and interests.* Through interactions with family members, adolescents often developed interests and recognised qualities about themselves. They also acknowledged the influence of family members on their current lives and future hopes.

4. *Mutual support.* The constancy of family members was reported to provide support during times of stress or illness. This appeared to be useful in helping the young people deal with stressful situations. Some participants also reported playing a supportive role themselves to family members.

5. *Guidance.* Parents were often named as models for behaviour or attitudes for participants. This included helping them to define their values and beliefs in relation to health and other attitudes about life.

6. *Memories and shared history.* Participants talked of memories of family members, sometimes those who have died. This seemed to be associated with a sense of connection and spirituality.

For parents, knowing about this ongoing valuing of their role can be helpful to keep them connected and engaged in the lives of their adolescents, particularly when they feel pushed away or excluded. It could be described as a parent–adolescent dance — moving in harmony and in tune with each other to the point that there is a moving forward and back as the young person's needs shift on a regular and ongoing basis. Knowing when to be there and when to back away, knowing how to approach conversations, when to attempt to open the door on a conversation and when to leave it for another time are crucial factors in this dance. This relationship, although more complex and outside of the total control of the parent, may not really be so different to the relationship that parents have developed from birth with their children — tuning in to the young child's needs, knowing when to be there to provide support and guidance, and when to step away to let them develop their own capacities. This is what you will have been doing since your child was born.

Dependence and independence

There is a paradox about parenting teenagers — the more they need us, the more they seem to push us away. Adolescence includes lots of changes, uncertainty and challenges in managing expectations when not knowing who they are really are. The search for identity that we've been hearing about for centuries requires a trying on of personas, testing ways of being, ways of looking and ways of seeing the world. This might be heightened now with the advent of social media, as this testing is recorded and publicly available (and open to critique) more than ever before. Adults and teenagers alike are trying to navigate this new space and find ways to make it work for us and not do harm.

It's within this context then that young people need to learn and be given opportunities to become independent, yet continue to be dependent on us as well. With the push for teenagers to stay at school and education programs longer, as well as economic pressures affecting the ability to move out of the family home, has come a greater dependency. It's not like the days when the option to leave school at 14 or 15 (like our parents and grandparents may have) meant going into an adult job, often a job for life. You can imagine in that scenario how the teenager needed to quickly adapt to an adult world, probably had access to support from adults outside of the home and could more easily move towards independence away from their own parents (perhaps with the support of a community of adults). Contrast that to a young person living at home studying into their 20s, perhaps balancing a part time job with study commitments, but having parents there trying to navigate this new adult/child space. It can sometimes be hard to see your teenager as the young adult they want to be when they're living at home and old habits prevail.

The playing out of this dependence–independence conundrum can be how parents can sometimes misinterpret and respond unhelpfully when a young person is trying to reach out for independence. As they push us away, we can take this personally and respond with emotion rather than more logically as we understand that this is part of their development. Having an open approach to forgiveness, taking time before responding and remembering that we are the adults can help us to prevent situations from escalating and hurtful conflicts occurring.

Reflection: Your teenagers' stage of development

- How would you describe your teenager's current stage of development?

- What developmental changes have you noticed over the last 3 months, 6 months, or year?

- What attitudes and behaviours do you see that are related to their stage of development?

- What do other parents say about their teenager's behaviour and attitudes at this age?

- What do you remember about yourself at your teenager's age?

- What did you need most at your teenager's age?

- What are three things you can do to help your teenager, taking into account what is going on for them at this time?

- How can you use technology as a way of connecting and strengthening your family's communication?

- In what ways does it help to know about adolescent development? What difference can it make to your day-to-day life?

- What are some examples of the paradox of parenting in your family at the moment — when does your teenager push you away while also still wanting you to be there? How do you typically respond? Are there other ways you can respond?

What's different about being a parent of a teenager compared to a parent of a younger child?

Parents are often very aware of the point when they realise that their child has become a teenager. There can be changes physically but they often talk about a shift in attitude and a pushing away from the parent that is quite tangible. This can start to happen before the parents are ready for it with signs starting to show up in late primary school when it feels like the child is not the same person as the one they knew before. This necessarily requires a shift in attitude from the parents if a good relationship is to be maintained. It's almost like starting to think again about how to parent. It's certainly a good time to reflect on what is going to be most important to you in the coming years, what values you will want to hold on to and what things you might be able to let go of. It's certainly a time for choosing your battles and keeping the focus on what really matters.

Trust and confidentiality

As part of the teenager's development, privacy and independence are important to them. This means that issues like trust and confidentiality are critical. If we want them to trust us we need to be able to respect their privacy and give them independence. We can very easily find ourselves in a situation where we are trying to help them but accidentally breach their trust. This becomes really important when teenagers are experiencing challenges because one of the barriers to young people reaching out to seek help from adults is a fear that the adults won't respect their confidentiality. It makes sense that they will want to own their personal information and decide who should know about it. They won't want their personal information to be shared without their knowledge and permission. They won't want people talking about them, even if the intentions of the person doing the talking are good and they are trying to help.

When I worked as a psychologist in schools I was always very aware of the risks of being in an environment where the needs of young people were discussed by staff. From an educational point of view this often made sense — knowing whether a student was away or at school, hearing about an issue between students, noticing when a student was having difficulties with learning or when a student's behaviour changed are all important within a caring and proactive school environment where teachers want to support their students and catch issues well before they escalate. In fact, these are usually protective actions which support students and can help students feel cared about. However, I also observed that there is a line that adults such as teachers and parents can cross sometimes where a young person can experience this sharing of information as a breach of trust. I was always conscious of this line and (in keeping with my ethical obligations also) worked hard to maintain confidentiality unless the young person had given me actual permission to share any information with certain people. Sometimes this related to potential risks or harm to them and I had to negotiate this agreement with them, knowing that if there were immediate risks I was obliged to disclose that anyway. Sometimes the young person was happy for me to share information with some adults, those they trusted. This was an important part of maintaining a good relationship with young people. Being respectful of their right to privacy was something that was always front of mind for me. This included even being seen talking to them in corridors or the school yard. I always checked in with them to make sure they were okay for this to happen and I always left it up to them to initiate the contact.

As a school psychologist, I worked in both primary and secondary schools and the differences were stark. In primary schools all the children wanted to come to see me or were happy to flock around me at recess and lunchtimes. They often asked if they could come to my groups or see me like other kids in their class. I think they loved the novelty of a different person to talk to. Adolescents on the other hand were often very polite and happy to talk to me but were much more guarded. I, as the adult, needed to be respectful of that and find ways to work that maintained the trust and independence that I knew was so important. This change in response is important for parents to be aware of too. What we do as parents when our children are younger will not be appropriate when they are teenagers. If we understand this as normal and healthy we will be able to adjust to this much better than if we view it as a rejection or as losing our ability to control them. It helps to focus on working on building a trusting relation-ship that encourages them to come to us, but also to help them be com-fortable in going to other trustworthy adults. This is a time when a village raising a child makes good sense. The more supportive adults a young person has around them the better they will be able to seek help and feel part of the community.

Learning to let go

Perhaps one of the aspects of being a parent of a teenager that causes the greatest angst is learning to let go. While instinctively we want to protect our children and in fact our life as a parent to this point has been all about keeping them safe and happy, we also need to learn to let them gradually become independent. In order to become independent, they need to separate from us. It's up to us to create an environment that will let them learn how to become independent. The timing of this is not simple and can't be prescribed simply by age. Letting them go too quickly or early can have repercussions, where they can find themselves in unsafe situations. Leaving it too late can mean they aren't learning the skills they require for their healthy development. Some kids are ready to become independent much earlier than others. Their personality and life experiences drive much of this. Some of this drive towards making their own decisions will be helpful for them in the longer term but can be risky when they are young. The job of the parent then is to help them to navigate this path. This typically involves placing boundaries where necessary while gradually loosening the reins so that they can test the waters for themselves. This is rarely an easy task, especially when some kids accept boundaries more easily than others.

It can be helpful to remember that parents bring their own personality and life experiences to the situation as well. For some parents letting go is difficult because they tend to be worriers, worrying about all the possible risks that their children might face. They might typically not take many risks in their own lives. This can play out in a number of ways with our kids. Some kids might take after their parents and also become worriers and non-risk takers. Other kids might rebel against that and seek out adventures and enjoy taking risks. When we haven't been risk-takers ourselves it can be hard to understand why they have this need, and it can be very hard to help them find ways to take risks in ways that are safe.

This idea of taking risks in safe ways can sound like an absolute contradiction, but it's all a matter of degree. There are some risks that have low possible implications and some risks that are more serious. It can often help to ask ourselves whether this will matter in five years' time. At times we also need to trust our kids — give them knowledge and skills as much as possible and then let them take the chance to test things out. Being there to support them as they need it is important — and the more trust they have in you the more likely they'll be to ask if help is required. Some people might argue that this navigation of life risks is essentially what life is all about — in fact it's what makes worth living. I'm reminded as I write this of the television advertisement (I think for a bank) where the couple sit in a café overlooking a beautiful seascape talking about ships being safe in the harbor, but that wasn't what they were built for. I think there's some truth in that idea for teenagers as much as we may want to keep them safe in the harbour.

Values

Sometimes when we have tensions and conflicts in our relationships with teenagers, it can be related to values. Values are essentially principles or standards of behaviour, often related to what we judge to be important in the way we live. The place of values in our conflicts may not always be obvious at first but if we break down the issues we can sometimes see the values more clearly. Adolescence is typically a time when young people challenge the ideas and assumptions made by their parents. It's part of their independence and ability to find their own identity separate from their family. Much of who we are as an individual relates to our values and how we put them into practice on a day-to-day basis.

It can be helpful to hear that while young people often go through periods of testing out our values and even rejecting, or rebelling against, them, quite often they will return to those values again as adults. As with other aspects of parenting teenagers if we trust that we have been influencing our kids for many years where our values have been on full display as we live them day in and day out, we will be in a better position to accept that our kids need to test them out for ourselves to make sure they fit. Sometimes we might also find that the testing of values by our teenagers encourages us to question those values. Perhaps they don't fit as well as we thought. We may have taken them on from our parents, taking them for granted rather than thinking about how they fit who we are now. Or perhaps the living out of the values can look different in various situations, or when there are a number of values in conflict or at stake. Teenagers can also often point out when we don't necessarily live up to our values. We might, for example, talk about values but not always behave in ways that are totally consistent with them. This can be challenging of course but if we see it as a chance to have a discussion about how values play out in the real world, it can be an enriching experience for us all.

Finding out more about values together can be helpful. You can explore values using the *Values in Action* web site: www.viacharacter.org. The web site includes an online 10-minute survey to discover character strengths and tools to help you use that information in your life.

Handling conflict

We often hear stories of the adolescent years being challenging because of conflicts between parents and teenagers. While it's normal for some conflict to occur when young people are testing boundaries and working out who they are, it's not always the case that conflicts are a big part of life for all parents of teenagers. This can be quite different to the way that conflicts were resolved, or avoided, when children were younger. We can often direct or distract younger children to manage or reduce conflicts.

Once our kids reach adolescence, they will want to have a stronger voice and fight for the things that matter to them. Of course, some younger children may have been doing this already and there mightn't be such a stark change during adolescence. The way we understand conflict will affect the way we view it and respond when it arises. If we struggle with conflict and see it as a negative part of life and even a failing because it breaks the harmony we hope to have in our families, we may be bothered by it. If, on the other hand, we see conflict as a normal and healthy way for people in the family to express different views and ways to do things, we will be able to focus on how to resolve the conflicts and learn about each other rather than trying to stop them.

In any social relationship, there is likely to be conflict to some degree so helping our kids learn the skills of respectful conflict resolution will be critical life skills that will equip them to deal with a whole range of social situations throughout their lives. Home is a testing ground for the development and practice of these skills. Seeing our interactions, even the most difficult ones, in this way can help us to feel more confident and normalise conflicts, rather than see them as our failures because everyone's not happy all of the time. This means we need to spruce up our conflict resolution skills too. In every conflict with our kids, we are modelling how to deal with it. They are learning from what we do as much as what we say. The family home can be a rich environment for practicing how to handle conflicts, beginning with small differences and tensions. Helping siblings to resolve conflicts in respectful ways can be a good starting point because you won't be so directly involved, will have some distance and can facilitate them to listen and respond to each other with care and respect. Conflicts are harder to resolve when your emotions are running high too.

It can be helpful for us to reflect on how we feel about conflict. If we typically confront issues head on, we will see conflict quite differently compared to someone who tries to avoid conflict at all costs. We might have one particular style of managing conflict or we may find that we respond differently depending on the situation. These ways of responding to conflict often began in our childhood in response to the ways that our parents dealt with conflict.

There is a point where conflict can get in the way of family functioning and it's important to monitor this and seek professional help if it feels like every discussion becomes a conflict and effective communication has broken down or when physical or emotional abuse or threats are involved. Conflict can also escalate where parents can feel unsafe with their teenagers. As we've seen, teenagers need a supportive family and conflict which is not managed effectively can get in the way of family members feeling safe and valued.

What caring looks like

As parents it's easy to think that we are always caring about our kids and that they know this because of all of the things we do and say. When children are younger they can easily take for granted the way that we care for them. When they head into adolescence, the way that caring looks might start to shift. As they push towards independence, they may be looking for less obvious caring from us. They might want to start doing things for themselves. Importantly too they might want to appear to be doing things for themselves. Parents often talk about the shift that occurs when kids no longer want a kiss goodbye when they're dropped at school. This can be experienced by parents as a rejection when for the child it's about them becoming more grown up and less dependent on parents. This doesn't mean that they don't want us to care about them. They just want us to do it differently and less obviously.

Looking out for signs like this can help us to recognise what they are needing from us. It might be that a gentle pat or smile can replace the kiss and they will be happy with that and we can still feel the connection that we have with them. This is an opportunity to tune into what they need while also recognising the importance of keeping the connection open and showing that we care in ways that they will be accepting of. This might be different for each of our children and continue to change over time. It's important to hold on to the idea that while they show that they don't want us to care or worry about them, they still need to know that we do care and that we are there for them. This is another strange paradox that we need to find a way to accept and understand if we want to maintain a close connection with our kids during adolescence.

Family dinners can be one of the most significant ways that a family can keep connected to each other, show that they care for each other and provide an important routine or ritual that can strengthen relationships. Research conducted in recent years has revealed the power of the family dinner as a way to promote family connectedness and enhance a range of positive outcomes for young people (Elgar, et. al., 2014). Importantly, this doesn't have to be every night but several nights a week has been shown to be effective.

The role of the school

It's tempting when our kids enter secondary school to feel like there's less of a role for us in their education. The secondary school environment is certainly very different to the primary school environment, even in schools where the early years of secondary school are included in the one setting. The shift towards content areas means that classes are set up differently and teachers have more specific training compared to the primary school teacher. Parents can experience the secondary school setting as a less welcoming place than a primary school setting where parents often hover and are encouraged to make themselves available to actively participate in their children's education. This can be deceiving because it suggests that there's no role for parents in their child's secondary schooling and that's simply not true. There is a need for a partnership to be developed with your child's secondary school but this will look different to what it did earlier. It's another circumstance where we need to find new ways to make and keep the connection with our child and their world.

There are many ways we can build the connection between home and school, beginning with how we ask our kids about their school day. We can continue to be curious about how their day went but we may need to find out about how their day is structured. Asking them to show you their timetable will help fill you in on the subjects they have each day and how the school day is structured. You can then tailor your questions around that. You might want to pay close attention to those subjects your child enjoys the most as well as those subjects they are most likely to struggle with. Keeping a focus on the positive will be important, particularly if your teenager is having some challenges with learning or settling in. Some teenagers relish the structure of secondary school and love engaging with new teachers and students, while others experience it as a confusing and potentially isolating environment. Having the timetable will also help you to prompt them to check that they have everything they will need for the day. Even though we could be tempted to think that this responsibility can end now that they're at secondary school, bear in mind that they will often still need help to get organised and to plan for their day. As they have many things to think about and manage, a gentle prompt about what subjects they have and what they need, along with the offer to help with anything they need, can help you to continue to feel like you have a role, but also let them know that you are interested, even though there is an expectation that they are becoming more capable and responsible for themselves.

Secondary schools can sometimes send different messages to young people about the level of responsibility they have. At times they expect teenagers to be responsible for themselves, yet when things go wrong they ring the parents and expect parents to take back that responsibility. Finding a way to navigate this so that there's shared responsibility between the young person, the school and the parent will be the best way to handle any challenges, but this can take quite a bit of effort and advocacy from parents to achieve. Kids will do best when parents and school staff are working together with the child/student at the centre. This means not undermining each other and providing a united front on important things like respectful and safe behaviour and commitment to learning. Remembering that you all have your child's wellbeing and success as your common goal will help to keep the focus on what matters most and avoid getting caught up in irrelevant discussions.

Reflection: Making sense of parenting for you at the moment

- What is working well with your parenting at the moment?

- How would you describe your family's strengths?

- What strengths does your teenager have that you can build on?

- What has changed in your family in the last 3 months, 6 months, 12 months?

- What are some of the decisions your teenager is now making? What works well to encourage them to make decisions for themselves?

- What do you find most difficult about letting go?

- What is it like for you when you see your kids making their own decisions?

- What are the ways you encourage your kids to take risks? What helps them to be safe enough?

- What are the values most relevant to your parenting role and your family? Which of your values clash with your teenager's values most at the moment?

- What values and strengths does your teenager have that you admire?

- What does conflict look like in your family? Does everyone get to speak their mind so that decisions can be made? Is there a tendency to avoid conflict? What can you do to encourage respectful conflict?

- What does caring look like to you? What would your teenager say caring looks like to him or her?

- Who are the adults you have allowed to be there alongside your family?

- What are the ways you support the school to work with you and your teenager?

Chapter 4

Understanding suicide

A s confronting as it is, gaining an understanding about suicide is important if we want to help someone who is feeling suicidal. Take care when reading this chapter, perhaps take some breaks or have someone handy who you can talk to.

Suicide is a complex phenomenon which occurs in a context influenced by many social, cultural, economic and psychological factors. The language of suicidality can be confusing and varies depending on who is talking about it, when and where. Suicidality is an overarching term which refers to all aspects related to suicide, including suicidal thoughts, plans, attempts and actual suicide. Suicide refers to death which was intended to end one's life. A suicide attempt refers to those acts aimed at ending life. Suicidal ideation (thoughts of suicide) can happen prior to the attempt. It's important to know, however, that many people have thoughts about suicide, but they don't all attempt suicide. Researchers are working hard to find out what makes a person go from thinking about suicide to acting on it. It's hard to know and likely to be a range of different factors. It's often thought that the suicidal person simply wants to end the pain and suffering they are feeling, rather than necessarily to end their life permanently. This is important to be aware of because it provides an opportunity to intervene. When time can be bought and a realistic solution can be found to their overwhelming problems and hope can be regained, the desire for suicide can subside or even disappear. Keeping a solution-focused lens while acknowledging the pain can be helpful. Seeking out the capacities and strengths of the person rather than focusing on the problems alone can send an important message that there is hope for the future.

Sometimes suicide attempts are referred to as self-harm and indeed acts associated with suicide are acts of harm to self. That may make sense, except there is also nonsuicidal self-injury/self-harm which is considered to be a separate, yet potentially related, act that is undertaken as a way of coping with distress. In the case of nonsuicidal self-injury, the person is not expressing a wish to die but rather to find a way to relieve the feelings they have. This is an important distinction but not always immediately apparent. Cutting, burning and hitting are examples of nonsuicidal self-injury. Recently we've been hearing about self-cyberbullying as another form. This involves people self-trolling and smearing their own reputations them-selves. It can be done by young people who appear to fit in, to have friends and are doing well at school. They may post something unkind about them-selves. Although research is limited, like other forms of self-harm it seems to be a way for young people to manage their feelings when struggling.

While people who engage in nonsuicidal self-injury may benefit from a response that is different to a person who is able to define dying as the goal of their hurting themselves, it is likely that these are not separate acts. We know that people who harm themselves are at increased risk of death by suicide. Although we're still understanding this connection, it's possible that they may accidentally kill themselves in the act of self-harming or at a different point in time their desire to die or not may shift. As they become accustomed to hurting themselves an act that goes a step further to hurt themselves more can potentially become a life-threatening act. Whether this is absolutely intended or not may be unclear.

One area of ambiguity which complicates the definition of suicide is the issue of intention. This is because the intentions of the suicidal person are not directly observable, and we can never be sure about the actual intention of another person. Following a suicide, there can be questions raised about whether the person was feeling suicidal but wanted to be found before they died or whether the person actually intended to die at all but may have died accidentally. When people die of apparent accidental causes there may be questions about whether there was an intention to die. This question of intention is open to interpretation and lacks scientific method as those who are investigating the cause of death may rely upon a post-death psychological autopsy where interviews with people known to the person and other information is gathered and analysed. Not everyone leaves a suicide note or talks about suicide before they die. This makes it very difficult for us to understand why people die by suicide and explains why there are so many efforts around the world to try to understand it better. It's difficult to stop something happening if we don't understand why it happens. Although there's a lot we still don't understand we do have growing knowledge and ideas and I'm keen to share those clues that can help parents to recognise the signs so they can act as early as possible.

Understanding suicidality as a response to distress that we can do something about will be helpful. If we see it as a way of responding to extreme pain and distress we can start to see a pathway through. We might be able to tap into the best of our parenting abilities to listen and help hold the pain our teenager is feeling. By believing that we can prevent suicide we will be more active and hopeful. Having a strong view about this will help our teenager. We need to be careful to balance this with understanding the extreme state of distress they are feeling. This is a sensitive balance.

Some theories about suicide

Researchers continue to look towards identifying underlying factors that may lead to suicide attempts and death by suicide. These factors include individual, family and community factors, particularly as it is clear from research that the risk of suicide varies in ways that relate to social, economic and demographic factors. For example, more men die from suicide than women (although more women attempt suicide than men) and Aboriginal and Torres Strait Islanders are at a higher risk of dying by suicide than non-Indigenous Australians. Trying to understand what leads to suicide and how to prevent it has occupied many researchers for a long time. Here are some of the most well known theories that serve to highlight the complexities of understanding suicide.

Durkheim's sociological theory

Sociological theories for understanding suicidal behaviour first began with the work of French social philosopher/sociologist Emile Durkheim in the late 19th century (1987). While Durkheim saw suicide as an act undertaken by an individual, he began to explore suicide as a social act impacted by social structures and social forces. He was interested in what happened when there was too much individualism within a society and also when there was too much social pressure. He saw social involvement (which included people feeling integrated within society as well as some regulation of their behaviours) as protection against suicide. According to this model, when people become disconnected from their social networks, their social supports are reduced and in turn suicide rates are likely to increase. This is particularly important for young people given the focus on social connections and the importance of being part of friendship groups, influenced by peers. It would be interesting to know what Durkheim would make of today's technological developments.

Shneidman's 'psychache'

Shneidman coined the term 'psychache' as the cause of suicide (1993). He described psychache as the hurt, anguish, soreness, aching, psychological pain in the psyche (the mind). He saw it as intrinsically psychological, including the pain associated with excessive shame, guilt, humiliation, loneliness, fear, and angst. He believed that suicide occurred when the psychache became unbearable for the individual. This varies between individuals with different individual thresholds for enduring psychological pain and a range of psychological needs that could be blocked and lead to psychache. In many ways this theory makes a lot of sense, particularly for teenagers who are experiencing many changes and challenges, some of them related to their developmental stage. It also recognises that people are affected differently by their experiences and therefore reach the threshold of psychache at different points.

O'Connor's integrated motivational–volitional model of suicidal behaviour

Rory O'Connor is a Scottish researcher who has been researching in the area of suicide for several decades (2018). In a recent visit to Australia, he spoke of how, despite his many years of research, we are still trying to make sense of when and why suicide is likely to occur. He has been working on a model that incorporates many of Durkheim and Schneidman's ideas. It is called the integrated motivational–volitional model (IMV model). O'Connor described his model as having three parts beginning with mapping the relationship between background factors and trigger events, the development of suicidal ideation, then suicidal intent and finally factors which actually lead to acts of suicidal behaviour. The model is helpful because it recognises the various factors which are pre-existing which may set the scene for difficulties which can be impacted by a range of other factors to lead to suicidal thoughts and intention before other factors come into play to lead to an act of suicidality. While the model can highlight the potential trajectory towards suicide, it also gives us pointers about the possible things that can come into play along the way to reduce the risk or prevent suicide from happening. It is a complex model but useful to show the many individual and social factors that come together to help us understand what might lead to suicidality. It highlights that suicide involves active decision-making by the individual within the context of stressful life events and circumstances.

Joiner's interpersonal–psychological theory of suicide

The interpersonal-psychological theory of suicide (IPTS) developed by Thomas Joiner and others (2005) focuses more on the factors which lead to suicide ideation and proposes that suicide ideation occurs due to the interaction of perceived burdensome and thwarted belongingness. According to the theory, the desire to die by suicide is not sufficient for lethal behaviour to occur. This is because individuals have a protective survival instinct and in order for suicide to occur they must lose some of the fear associated with death. The researchers suggest that it is possible to acquire the capability for suicide through habituation or getting used to the idea. This could be why previous suicide attempts (and self-harm) are such serious risk factors for future suicide.

This theory includes a focus on belongingness that is of particular relevance to teenagers. When the need to belong is unmet, referred to in the theory as thwarted belongingness, a desire for death develops. It also recognises that thwarted belonging is multidimensional, including the need for positive interactions with the same individuals over the long-term as well as reciprocally-caring relationships. Adolescence is developmentally a period where these interactions are often challenging and young people are trying to find where they fit and how to develop relationships with others. Feeling isolated or left out can be extremely difficult for teenagers. This is why it's important to recognise the importance of friendships in the lives of teenagers.

The other aspect of the model is the idea of perceived burdensomeness where a person feels that they are a burden on others, often their family. They may develop the view that their family would be better off if they were dead. Two aspects of this have been described — the belief that the self is so flawed as to be a liability on others and affectively-laden cognitions or thoughts of self-hatred. These are powerful feelings that the young person experiences and closely related to their sense of self-worth. In such a situation, they can easily interpret things we say as being a burden on parents and other family members so our communication needs to be closely monitored and communication kept open to explain that they are a valued member of the family and not a burden. Knowing this can help us to more clearly outline concerns and ensure we follow up after arguments or times where the young person may have felt criticised. Even asking for help can seem like a burden for a young person so it's important that we are clear that we are not burdened by helping them.

Wasserman and others

The Wasserman model (2012) is useful to help us understand what might be leading up to the risk of suicide by a focus on the trajectory towards or away from suicidal behaviour. It particularly focuses on both observed and non-observed behaviours, where a person might be thinking about suicide for some time before it is obvious to others. According to this model, the behaviour might journey between observable and non-observable over time as different life events occur. Importantly, it also notes that suicidal processes can decline and subside due to the development of individual coping and treatment strategies. This is of course critically important and necessary for us to be aware of.

The silencing of suicidal behaviour is particularly relevant to teenagers given their need for privacy and independence. You can imagine young people keeping their suicidal thoughts to themselves until they build up and become obvious. This also highlights the importance of adults around young people being in tune with what is happening for them so that they can notice the behaviours as early as possible and ideally have a trusting relationship so that the issues leading to the non-observable behaviours can be brought to the surface and dealt with in ways that will reduce the risk of suicide.

It seems likely that often suicidal thoughts are not communicated. We may only become aware of them when the thoughts or behaviours erupt above the line of visibility. The suicidal thoughts (or ideation) can be bubbling away under the surface for some time without being able to be observed by anyone else. These thoughts may come and go and may even reduce over time. They may continue and build up and become visible to others, through being spoken about or through behaviours that we might observe. This might be efforts to talk about how they feel or behaviours that show the distress. It may present as a suicide attempt before it's observed. This may lead to some actions, such as treatment or problem solving that is helpful, and the suicidal thoughts may subside again. This may mean the situation is resolved or it may mean that the suicidal thoughts and behaviours re-emerge again and the pattern continues.

For me, the Wasserman model is both hopeful in bringing to light the opportunities that arise for us to intervene, but at the same time incredibly confronting as we recognise that there's so much that can be going on below the surface before it's noticed by others. It reminds us of the possibility of death by suicide — but also the possibility of intervening to prevent suicide. If we are going to support young people, we need to face both of these possibilities, obviously prioritising finding ways of preventing suicide. But to do that we have to face the prospect that the young person could die by suicide. There's not much that could confront us more as parents.

Hawton's theory on adolescent self-harm and suicide

Hawton and colleagues describe self-harm and suicide in adolescence as the end-product of a complex interplay between genetic, biological, psychiatric, psychological, social and cultural factors (2012). His model brings together many of the risk and protective factors and shows how these come together over time to lead to a possible risk of suicide or self-harm.

The researchers state that psychosocial stressors, especially relationship problems, are frequent precipitants for suicide in adolescents. This is likely to be particularly true in those younger than 14 years, when suicide often follows a brief period of stress, and psychiatric disorder is less common. They suggest that life chart approaches to investigating youth suicide suggest three groups:

1. Those with longstanding life and behavioural problems, school failure, family relationship problems, childhood sexual abuse, family violence, personality problems, low self-esteem, and poor peer relationships

2. Those with major psychiatric disorder (including two subgroups— individuals with a protracted suicidal process and those with a brief suicidal process)

3. Those in whom the suicidal process occurred as an acute response to life events.

Emotional pain communication model — Dunkley and others

Understanding the meaning underlying the suicidal thoughts and behaviour will help parents work out how to respond. This requires the ability to notice and listen to the clues that young people are sending. A recent study by Dunkley and others (2018) conducted in the United Kingdom identified four ways that messages of suicidality can be spoken or heard — or not. Although the study looked at therapy settings, I think the four categories are useful for parents to think about as well:

- *Type 1: Unspoken/unheard.* When emotional pain is neither spoken by the patient nor recognised by the professional; for example, where a patient deliberately withholds communication.

- *Type 2: Spoken/unheard.* When emotional pain is expressed by the patient, but they perceive that this message remains unheard; for example, when a patient's phone call has not been returned.

- *Type 3: Spoken/heard.* When emotional pain is spoken and the patient perceives that the message has been heard; for example, when a staff member is visibly moved by the patient's plight.

- *Type 4: Unspoken/heard.* When emotional pain remains unspoken, but the mental health professional detects this and allows the patient to feel heard; for example, when the patient's out-of-character behaviour alerts a staff member to their pain.

This reminds us that communication is never just verbal. Young people may be trying to communicate how they're feeling without saying the words. In fact it can be very difficult to find the words to express exactly how we feel, even as adults. Imagine how challenging it is to say that you feel like you want to die. We know from Kids Helpline research conducted by Your Town (2018) that children and young people are in fact trying to tell adults how they feel and they don't always get heard. So they are speaking the words or believe that they are communicating their feelings, but their messages are being dismissed or ignored. It's likely that this exacerbates the negative feelings they have and could place them at even greater risk.

As parents then there are two main points to this:

1. Finding ways to be in tune with our kids is critical if we want to notice the unspoken messages they send

2. We also need to take notice and hear the spoken words, taking them all seriously and acting accordingly.

In my work with parents, I've often heard them talk about a 'gut feeling' or a sense that something is wrong even if they can't put their finger on what this is. Perhaps this is when the body language and unspoken messages are present without the words. I always encourage parents to tune into this and create opportunities for young people to feel safe and comfortable to express and share their feelings. Helping them to find ways to express their suicidal thoughts and feelings and being ready and open to hearing them is critical if we want to support kids who are feeling suicidal. It's only then that we can really help.

Bringing all the theories together — What might make a person thinking about suicide act on it?

This may well be the most important question we can ask, and certainly a focus of much research around the world at the moment. The best response we currently have probably comes from the O'Connor IMV model mentioned earlier. He outlines the following factors that sit between suicidal ideation and intent and actual suicidal behaviour:

- Access to means — does the individual have ready access to likely means of suicide?

- Planning (if–then plans) — has the individual formulated a plan for suicide?

- Exposure to suicide or suicidal behaviour — has a family member/friend engaged in suicidal behaviour?

- Impulsivity — does the individual tend to act impulsively or on the spur of the moment?

- Physical pain sensitivity/endurance — has the individual high (increased) physical pain endurance?

- Fearlessness about death — is the individual fearful about death/has this changed?

- Mental imagery — does the individual describe visualising dying or after death?

- Past suicidal behaviour — has the individual a history of suicide attempts or self-harm?

Looking out for these could give you a focus when concerned about your teenager and also help you to focus your conversations. While it can be confronting to talk about these topics, it could be reassuring for your teenager to know that you are open to having the conversation and the silence can be lifted.

Chapter 5

Suicide risk and protective factors and warning signs

Common myths about suicide

The gaps in our knowledge about why suicide happens has been apparent for decades and longer. When we don't understand something, humans seem to have an innate tendency to try to make sense of it and sometimes these can be later proven to be incorrect. This is certainly the case for suicide, and some of these incorrect ideas are important to know about (see Table 5.1).

Risk and protective factors

Current ideas around suicide prevention often draw upon a risk and protective factors framework which include a wide range of factors which influence suicidality. Risk factors increase the likelihood of suicidal behaviour while protective factors are related to a person's ability to cope with difficult circumstances and may reduce the likelihood of suicidal behaviours. A number of theories draw upon this framework. For example, risk factors

Table 5.1 Myths and facts about suicide

Myth	Fact
Asking someone if they are suicidal will give them the idea.	There is no evidence that talking to someone about suicidal thoughts is harmful. You can ask the person directly if they are feeling suicidal or if they have been thinking about suicide. This gives the person the message that they can talk openly and honestly about suicide. Often young people can be having thoughts of suicide but not share them with anyone. Letting them know you are interested and it's okay to talk about these thoughts can be the first step in helping them work out what they need.
It's my fault they are suicidal.	It is not anyone's fault that a person is feeling suicidal. Suicide is a complex phenomenon with many different things contributing to a person's risk. These may have built up over a period of time or it could be that the person's perceptions of how things are have become negative and they are feeling hopeless. There are things you can do that will be helpful and supportive.
There are no warning signs that someone may be suicidal.	Although we sometimes hear that people weren't aware of any warning signs when a person dies by suicide, there are often warning signs. A person who is thinking about suicide will usually give some clues or signs to those around them that indicates that they are distressed. These might be physical signs (e.g. tiredness) or behavioural changes (e.g. angry outbursts, becoming withdrawn). Sometimes there will be more obvious signs like saying that their life is not worth living or they'd be better off dead.
If someone talks about suicide, they probably don't intend to follow through with it.	If someone talks about suicide or hurting themselves, they are more likely to be trying to make sense of their experience or reaching out for help. Any talk of suicide should be taken seriously and questions asked about what the person is thinking and whether they have a plan to kill themselves. Thoughts of suicide are common and don't necessarily mean that a person is going to act on the thoughts but it's important that they are not dismissed or ignored.

Table 5.1 continued over page ...

Table 5.1 ... continued

Once a person feels suicidal, they will always feel that way.	Suicidal thoughts are not necessarily permanent. An increased risk of suicide is often short-term and may be related to a particular situation. Being able to resolve the situation and getting help with any underlying issues can mean that a person may not feel suicidal again. Sometimes suicidal thoughts can become chronic if the issues remain unresolved.
Only people diagnosed with mental health disorders are suicidal.	Not everyone who is suicidal has a diagnosed mental health disorder. Many people with mental health disorders are not affected by suicidal behaviour.

have been described in explanatory models of suicide, such as the stress-diathesis model (van Heeringen, 2012). This model recognises that stressful life events can be triggers of suicidal behaviour. It is also noted that many people experience stress and negative life events but these do not always lead to suicidal behaviour, even when extreme stress is present. The stress-diathesis model therefore considers the development of suicidal behaviour involving a vulnerability as a risk factor predisposing an individual to such behaviour when stress is encountered. The model is useful in the identification of suicide risk and preventing suicidal behaviour, however, further research is still required to gain a better understanding of how the stress and diathesis components relate to each other.

While risk and protective factors can be useful in understanding what factors appear to come together to increase the likelihood that suicide will occur, the framework works best when it's used at a population level. This is when we can see patterns and factors which come together for large numbers of people which indicate that these are likely to be factors related to suicide. However, people are not that simple and at an individual level these factors may or may not be helpful. Risk and protective factors often interact in complex ways so that they don't operate in isolation. For example, knowing that males are at greater risk of dying of suicide whereas women tend to attempt suicide more. This seems to be related to the methods used to die with males tending to use more lethal means. Knowing about the differences between males and females doesn't give us anything that useful when we are concerned about our own teenager. We need to be equally worried about them both if they are suicidal. At a population level though we might see programs or activities that target males and females differently.

More than 200 risk factors have been identified as potentially related to suicide risk. Important risk factors include:

- Past suicide attempts (This is the major risk factor for suicide. Risk is highest during the initial week after the suicide attempt and remains high during the following year after the attempt.)

- Family history of suicide

- Impulsive behaviour

- Relationship breakdowns

- History of substance abuse

- Access to lethal means

- Difficult life events

- History of mental illness

- History of physical or sexual abuse

- History of childhood trauma

- Having a terminal or chronic illness or pain

- Experience of bullying

- Loss of someone close to them

- Loss of someone they connect to who died by suicide

- Exposure to suicidal behaviour of others

- Exposure to sensational media reporting about suicide deaths

- Social isolation.

You will have noticed from this very big list that some of these risk factors relate to circumstances from the past that can't be changed (e.g., experiences of abuse or loss that happened in the past) although we may be able to provide support to help people manage the effects of those circumstances. Other risk factors are much more current and may be changeable. Looking for ways to resolve current problems which may be related to previous life experiences can be helpful. For example, for people who have experienced abuse or significant losses in childhood, it can be useful to learn about how this may be impacting on life now or potentially place them at risk of suicide (or other issues). Counselling support or specific treatment for trauma or grief can be helpful to make sense of these experiences and reduce their current impact. Learning how to recognise signs and triggers related to those experiences and knowing what to do to manage them will form part of this work and mental health professionals can be very helpful.

Protective factors are more pliable and can be increased. Many of the ideas in this book are actually aimed at building protective factors (e.g., increasing support networks, developing coping skills). Protective factors include:

- Social support and connectedness in stable relationships

- Balanced physical health

- Having plans for the future

- Engaging in meaningful activities and sense of purpose

- Strong reasons for living

- Access to and availability of effective mental health care

- Life skills (problem solving, coping skills and adaptability to change)

- Cultural beliefs that discourage suicide

- Religious beliefs that discourage suicide.

Some of these protective factors will be present already and you'll be able to recognise them in your teenager. Others might get you thinking about what can be done to develop them. A good example of one that can be developed is life skills. Schools may be working on these through social and emotional learning curriculum or programs but this requires support from home as well. Protective factors can give us hope because we can work on these to help the young person build confidence and increase capacities to reduce suicide risk.

Warning signs

One of the other useful things for you to know about are warning signs. These are the signs that have been found to be indicators that a person might be at increased risk of suicide. This has often been discovered during psychological autopsies by a coroner after deaths by suicide. Some of the warning signs can be common in adolescence or may indicate a mental health problem with or without suicidality, so there's quite a bit to sort out when you look at this list. I've included many of the signs so that you can be fully aware and know what to look out for. It's important to know that these signs don't always lead to a person attempting suicide but should nevertheless be taken seriously. At a minimum, they could be indicating that something is wrong.

Knowing about these signs can prompt you to keep taking notice and talking with your teenager to ensure the door to sharing concerns and getting help is always wide open. Remember that people show their signs differently. Some signs will be verbal and some non-verbal. They may be extremely subtle. Knowing your teenager and noticing even small changes can mean you are prepared to have a conversation about those changes at the earliest possible time. Tune into your gut feelings but try to also identify behaviours of concern. Raising those behaviours with your teenager will give you something tangible to focus on. Bear in mind also that young people are wanting to have privacy and trying to be independent. The way you ask about how they are needs to take this into account and respect their need to be treated as a young person and not like a child.

One of the most confusing signs to look out for is when a previously distressed and suicidal person suddenly becomes happier. This can be because they have made a plan to die and feel relieved. It's the sudden shift that you notice and naturally you may well be pleased to see them looking happier. This can be difficult to see as a warning sign at the time and often parents can instead see it as a sign that the young person is overcoming their difficulties and will be okay. It will help to keep the conversations happening while trying to read nonverbal signs and cues as well as what the young person is actually saying.

Other warning signs to look out for beginning with those most obvious to suicide:

- Searching about suicide on the internet

- Gathering materials (pills, ropes or a weapon)

- Talking about killing themselves — active ('I'm going to kill myself') or passive ('I wish I could go to sleep and not wake up' or 'I wouldn't mind being hit by a bus')

- Mentioning or joking about suicide, death or dying

- Not wanting to exist

- Giving away possessions or writing a will, suicide note or goodbye letter

- Returning to places where people have died or where they are remembered

- Feeling like their life has no purpose, is hopeless or there is no future (e.g., saying 'There's nothing to live for', 'There's no point')

- Feeling distraught, helpless and not able to see a way out of their problems (e.g., saying 'I've had enough, there's nothing I can do')

- Feeling like a burden (e.g., saying 'you'd be better off without me')

- Feeling damaged

- Looking for escape (e.g., saying 'I just want to get away from everything')

- Feeling alone and unsupported (e.g., saying 'No-one understands'. 'No-one cares'.)

- Self-harming (e.g., cutting, burning)

- Feeling depressed

- Emotional outburst or unexplained crying

- Lack of interest in activities once enjoyed

- Changes in sleep

- Changes in eating

- Changes in energy levels

- Loss of interest in personal appearance and hygiene

- Irritability, being moody or easily upset
- Shame or humiliation
- Mood swings
- Feeling stuck (e.g., saying 'There's nothing that I can do')
- Not communicating with family and friends
- Reckless behaviours, risk taking, fighting or breaking the law
- Increased drug and alcohol use
- Decreased academic or work performance.

Parents of teenagers may not be aware of their teenagers' suicidality. In a recent study in Philadelphia in the United States, 5,000 young people aged 11 to 17 years and their parents found that among the teenagers who reported that they had thought about taking their own life, 50% of their parents said they had no idea (Jones, et. al., 2019). Interestingly, young people in the study downplayed reports of their thoughts compared to what parents saw as troubling indications. A significant number of teenagers denied that they had thoughts of suicide or death even though their parents told the researchers they had. The researchers also commented on a tendency for some parents to find it difficult to face the thought that their teenager was suicidal, what they termed the 'not-my-kid' syndrome. This study highlights the importance of parents being open to the idea that their kids may have suicidal thoughts, knowing about warning signs and the need for open and ongoing communication between parents and teenagers.

Chapter 6

What do we know about youth suicide?

What does research tell us about young people in Australia and suicide?

The issues around youth suicide began to be addressed in Australia with the appointment of the Youth Suicide Prevention Advisory Group by the Commonwealth Department of Human Services and Health in 1995 (Mitchell, 2000). Youth suicide continues to be prioritised as suicide attempts and deaths continue to occur. It's difficult to know the extent of suicidal behaviours among young people. It's likely that it's not something that young people share with adults and research has limitations because many suicide injuries and attempts are not recorded (such as when a young person doesn't attend hospital).

The main source of data that tells us about the extent of suicidality amongst young people is the Australian Bureau of Statistics (ABS) annual data. In the most recent data available, the ABS reported that 100 children and young people (61 males and 39 females) aged between 5 and 17 years died of suicide in 2018 (Australian Bureau of Statistics, 2019). Importantly, 78% of deaths occurred between the ages of 15 and 17 years, but clearly younger young people and children can and do die by suicide sometimes.

Research that gives us another perspective comes from the Kids Helpline (Your Town, 2016). The Helpline has collected data for many years and recently pulled together a report looking at suicide and self-harm. This data alarms me for a number of reasons. Firstly, the age of children calling the Helpline in relation to suicide is younger than most people might expect — children as young as seven have rung them having suicidal thoughts and even having a plan. Secondly, and most alarming to me, is that they report not feeling supported by adults, even when they tell them. If anything spurred me on to write this book, this is it. To think that children and young people are trying to tell us, the adults in their lives, how they feel and we are not hearing them or helping them, is dispiriting. I'm not saying this is intentional on the part of those adults, but I do think we need to know about this and we need to be better prepared and open to hearing what is going on for these kids. Thankfully, we have the Kids Helpline to be there and these children and young people have the courage, and skills, to ring them and share their distress with them.

What might lead up to a suicide attempt by a young person?

Now that you've read about some of the theories related to suicidality you might have ideas about what might lead up to a suicide attempt by a young person. You might be thinking that there could be a lot of things that are brewing for a while and build up with one last straw, such as an argument or relationship breakup, when the suicide risk increases. Or you might be thinking that there's still so much that we don't know about suicide that it mightn't happen like that at all. A young person who is impulsive might become suicidal quite quickly and there might not have been a whole lot of things happening beforehand but rather a sudden build-up of issues with the young person becoming overwhelmed and not able to find another solution. A young person who is struggling with problem solving (and remember that the brain is changing during adolescence which makes it harder for young people to easily make decisions) may find it impossible to develop a practical plan to manage difficult situations. If they are isolated from adults who can help them, or don't want to ask anyone for help, it's easy to see how they may spiral into a path where suicide looks like the only response to their situation.

You might be wondering how young people who seem to have so much to live for could even think about suicide. You might have thoughts about how kids these days have it so easy compared to when you were growing up. All of these thoughts can make sense to us and remind us how hard it is for us to understand what is happening for another person. Sometimes our own experiences and awareness, however, don't help to explain what's going on for others. Again, the adolescent experience is complex and ways that we see the world may not be the same for them.

A recent study completed in the United States after a series of suicide clusters across four counties provides us with some useful insights (Colorado Office of the Attorney General, 2018). The researchers break the study findings into risk and protective factors related to suicidality and included young people, parents and other adults such as teachers and health professionals in the study. Here's some of their key findings along with my thoughts about how this might be relevant in Australia:

- Unemployment and a struggling economy were identified as the risk factors most raised across the four counties. This can relate to not having access to health insurance and availability of prosocial activities, particularly in rural areas. We know that these are risk factors for young people in Australia too, with social and economic determinants of health related to increased suicide risk. Not being able to access mental health support is an issue for many Australians.

- Pressure and anxiety about academic performance and in extracurricular activities, including feeling that expectations placed on young people were unrealistic and young people were not given the tools to manage the pressure in a healthy way. Young people expressed that they are also managing information overload via the internet and social media, and other stressors such as school shootings, relationships and sex, divorce and substance use. Both young people and adults stated that young people have no time to decompress and to take a break for their brains, especially with bell-to-bell instruction in most schools and the pace of extra-curricular activities. These concerns have also been flagged in Australia, particularly in relation to the pressures caused by NAPLAN beginning in primary school and culminating in ATAR scores in year 12. While thankfully Australia doesn't have the experience of school shootings that the United States has, nevertheless the significant experiences of family and community violence here shouldn't be underestimated in its effects on young people in Australia. The busyness of Australian families has also been commented on by psychologists and others in recent years.

- The use of social media and technology was identified as a risk factor for young people. More specifically, the report listed cyberbullying, the loss of interpersonal social skills and an inability to take a break from constant interaction, particularly negative interaction, on social media as risks. Many expressed a concern that adults do not know how to navigate the technological world of youth, and therefore don't know how to help young people build resiliency around it. Other concerns related to young people being exponentially more exposed to opportunities to be impacted by the emotional lives of their peers, making managing the spread of harmful information impossible. Young people also expressed feelings of anxiety about their image that must be maintained on social media, and that mistakes they make feel magnified on social media. We've heard a lot of about these potential impacts of technology in Australia too and there is currently a lot of effort being directed towards helping parents and other adults learn about technology and its impacts. It is clear from this list of concerns from both young people and adults that the pervasive nature of technology cannot be minimised and that adolescent development and behaviour increasingly cannot be understood without the context of technology taken into account.

- Perceived lack of coping skills and resilience among youth. This was described as young people not being able to cope after experiencing difficulties such as the loss of a relationship or not achieving something in school. This comes up often in Australia too and I struggle with the nature of this for a number of reasons. Firstly, it has a judgement about it, sounding like something adults say about young people in a critical way, secondly because it's pretty simplistic particularly taking into account the issues related to technology that face young people and lastly because I see resilience as not just about an individual having the coping skills. Instead I see that for children and young people (and adults too!) resilience is also about the way that supports are there to help them during difficult times. Of course, young people need to develop coping skills and resilience to deal with the many challenges they face in daily life, but I think we need to look a whole lot deeper into what helps these to develop over time, taking into account all the developmental challenges we've talked about, and what role adults like parents and teachers play in helping young people be prepared for and able to deal with challenges that arise. Perhaps young people are feeling the pressure to cope alone rather than sharing this with others, or perhaps as parents have been worried about their kids they have tended to be protective and not encouraged kids to learn how to deal with small disappointments along the way. Perhaps young people are dealing with issues in ways that weren't the same as in the past. For example, a failure at school or a relationship breakdown is no doubt much more public now due to social media so there can be much at stake. New coping skills may need to be developed in order to deal with these kinds of scenarios — for young people and adults alike.

- Effects of being exposed to adult suicides and/or of having a family member die by suicide was also included as a risk factor. This was described in the study as a significant concern with youth suicide having a profound effect on their communities. Community members in the study talked about tension, worry, fear, devastation, shock, confusion, paralysis, exhaustion, urgency, desperation and surrendering and flight in relation to this. Some of them spoke of concerns that suicide was beginning to be seen as normal in their communities with some people saying that suicide had become a conceivable option, as they believed that if others couldn't get help to prevent their suicide they might also not be able to get help for themselves either. Parents, who did not feel prepared to deal with such a significant issue and professionals, including school staff, reported feelings of fear, compassion fatigue and feeling in a constant state of crisis. There's a lot about this topic obviously that is also very relevant in Australia. Concerns in relation to the impact of knowing people who have died by suicide has certainly been recognised in Australia as a critical risk factor for young Aboriginal and Torres Strait Islanders because the rate of death by suicide of Aboriginal and Torres Strait Islanders is much higher than non-Indigenous Australians. The issue of contagion has also been recognised in Australia particularly amongst young people who are so strongly influenced by peers and other significant people to them. This can extend to celebrities and other people who they don't actually know personally. It seems that it's not only a personal relationship that is important but also a sense of connection, or of somehow being like that person, that can lead to risks of contagion.

- Some people included in the study responded that they felt as though many parents do not believe or recognise the suicide risk for their children. One of the suggestions made in the study related to more training for adults and parents about how to talk with children and young people about suicide. Importantly, the youth focus group participants in the study felt that adults' responses when there has been a suicide is confusing and inadequate. The young people reported that they wanted to have an authentic relationship with adults so they could connect and feel comfortable but sensed that adults were fearful of saying the wrong thing, resulting in no conversations about suicide at all or an intense reaction where young people felt like they were being interrogated about their own personal suicidality. The young people also reported that they felt like they were expected to act like adults and perform like adults, yet they were not always treated as adults or given credit for being capable of handling frank discussions about difficult issues like suicide. I've talked about this a lot so far and reading this report affirms for me the reason for writing this book.

- Stigma and taboos of suicide and mental health issues were reported along with the pressure for parents and young people to appear perfect with a feeling that no-one is allowed to show they have problems. There were also some reports of a strong culture of secrecy and not sharing problems outside of the family unit. My experience as a psychologist and also in writing this book would support these ideas in Australia too. While there have been considerable efforts to reduce the stigma of suicide and mental health issues in Australia for the last decade or more, I'm aware that many parents can be struggling with concerns in relation to their teenager's mental health and suicidality without sharing these with others. I saw this often in parenting groups and I've had many people disclose their concerns and experiences to me when I tell them in conversation about writing this book.

- Lack of connection to a caring adult was identified as a concern in the community focus groups. Youth participants described a deep desire to have authentic relationships with adults. They stated that when they discuss difficult topics, they do not often experience these interactions as authentic or helpful. They are concerned that adults will 'freak out' or overreact and not listen. They stated that they wished adults could just be with them in their pain without jumping to assessments or solutions, but rather just try to understand. They also expressed frustration that adults, most often parents, tended to minimise their problems and pain. They felt disheartened when adults told them to speak up about issues that concern them, but then shut them down when they do raise their voice. When they have established relationships with trusted adults, they reported that they will go to those adults for support. Building that trust requires time and a willingness and capacity to talk with young people about difficult subjects. This has been highlighted in Australia too with consistent messages for parents and teachers that building a strong and trusting relationship with children and young people is the most protective thing we can do for their mental health and wellbeing.

- Judgement and lack of acceptance in the community of those who do not fit with the dominant community norms. Young people explained that some people were afraid to be who they are and that they are growing up in a culture of harsh judgement, belittling and lack of acceptance, let alone tolerance. In particular, these concerns were raised about a lack of community acceptance of young people who identify as LGBTQI. In Australia, we see examples of this lack of acceptance on a day-to-day basis and of course in 2017 we were confronted by the same sex marriage debates. We can all play a role in building acceptance and encouraging this in our kids. Our modelling of acceptance will not only encourage our kids to do this but also help them to feel more accepted by us, particularly if they feel like they are different to us or our ideas of what they should be like.

- Substance use, mental health disorders, trauma history and availability of mental health care. Substance use and abuse by young people and carers, along with depression and anxiety, were commonly discussed risk factors contributing to suicidal behaviour in young people. These were described as generational in scope yet because of stigma and challenges in accessing mental health supports, they often go underdiagnosed and undertreated. Challenges of being able to access the right service at the right time were also identified. These are all factors relevant to Australia as well, with a number of reviews currently underway to look at how to improve the mental health system to improve access and treatment. The impact of intergenerational trauma has been recognised in Aboriginal and Torres Strait Islander families as well as in families impacted by complex or developmental trauma (such as childhood sexual abuse). The importance of the family as a significant influence on young people means that any experiences of trauma or distress on previous family members can flow on to children and young people in future generations.

- Protective factors included school-related supports, extracurricular activities, various suicide prevention and intervention efforts, increased collaborative efforts of public health departments and increased co-operation across resources. It was noted that these varied across the counties with less availability in rural areas and in some cases not all activities were open to all young people. This sounds similar to efforts in Australia. We know that young people who are engaged at school and with activities that are meaningful for them will feel supported and the risk of suicide may be reduced.

- Church/faith-based activities were identified as protective factors, particularly in relation to youth-focused activities and spaces for interpersonal interaction and positive activities. This may well be the case in Australia too although we also know that increasingly there's a move away from traditional religions. There were also concerns raised in relation to faith-based organisations promoting stigma toward suicide and not being considered accessible by all young people, for example LGBTI young people.

- Natural resources were also identified as a protective factor that is underutilised by families and institutions, sometimes because of geographic accessibility and transportation. There's been a recent push in Australia for us to get back to nature, particularly for younger children. This is largely related to a lack of balance in our lives with concerns in relation to technology use and risks of physical health impacts, such as obesity.

Reading through this list reminded me of some work I did as a project worker a long time ago to try to prevent chroming (sniffing inhalants) by young people in a community in the western suburbs of Melbourne. We talked with young people in an area where this was happening a lot and asked them why they thought this was happening in their community. I distinctly remember two main reasons they gave us — boredom and to deal with emotional pain. Some of the kids were disconnected from families and schools and hung around the streets together, shoplifting spray paints and going to their favourite isolated spot to use it, either by themselves or with their friends. Other kids saw them doing this and copied so it took off in the area. Hearing what the young people told us helped the community group I worked with to come up with a whole range of ideas. Many of these ideas were obvious and relatively easy to implement — beginning with working with traders to reduce accessibility of the spray paints (like locking them away so that customers had to ask for them and couldn't steal them) and working with the local Council and police to increase opportunities for activities to reduce the boredom. Finding ways to support young people with their emotional pain was much more difficult to develop simple strategies for. Trying to find ways to prevent the struggles kids were going through, helping them to access mental health services, and keeping them connected with schools who could provide support and trying to help their families (or other carers because some of them were disconnected from families) to understand and support them needed a more comprehensive plan. There were two main learnings from that project for me — firstly, we need to listen to the people affected to understand what is happening for them and then we need a multipronged approach to tackle whatever it is they can tell us. I think this relates also to supporting kids who are suicidal.

Not knowing exactly what causes the situation where a young person becomes suicidal can be unsettling. It can feel that it's impossible to stop something if we don't know what the cause is. However, we do know that there are some things that can make an immediate difference like reducing access to means (e.g. locking knives away, removing medications from easy access). Recognising the warning signs as early as possible and asking about suicide can encourage the person to talk about how they're feeling. Getting help for any possible mental health issue can be an important way to improve the way the person is able to cope and may reduce the risk of suicide. These are all things that parents can do.

What might this mean for your teenager?

As you read this you may have a number of different responses. We could see these responses on a continuum from 'this would never happen to my teenager/not my kid' to 'there is a very real risk that this could happen to my teenager any time'. I would be thinking that you are probably somewhere in the middle or at the real risk end of this continuum because you're reading this book. As you've recognised some of the risk factors or warning signs, your place on the continuum might have shifted, perhaps more than once. At the risk of sounding alarmist, I am keen to raise your awareness of the possibility of suicide risk for your teenager. It's only when adults around a young person take this risk seriously that we can really be helpful to them. If we are busy reassuring ourselves or minimising the signs that we are seeing, we are of no help, and potentially can be doing harm if the young person is trying to reach out to us. This approach can silence the young person, leaving them isolated and potentially more at risk. Remember they might be reaching out to us in subtle ways, perhaps testing the water to see how we react, to see if we are safe people to talk to about how they're feeling. If you have a gut feeling that there is something going on, tune into that and trust that you know your teenager well enough so you're likely to pick up on tiny messages they are sending.

It might be helpful to think about suicide thoughts, plans or attempts in a couple of ways:

- As a way of experiencing and/or communicating the depths of despair (or frustration, hurt, helplessness and many other possible emotions) the young person is feeling; and/or

- As a refuge or a last resort when it feels impossible to cope any longer.

This may occur within the context of a mental health problem and getting that addressed will be important. However, by understanding more about the suicidal experience we can respond better. With both of these situations there are ways we can help — beginning with listening and showing the young person that we hear their distress and want to be there with them to work out how to get through this difficult time. Seeing this as human need at its most extreme, rather than as dysfunction, can help you to feel confident entering into this space as a helper or support person. Trusting that being there will make a positive difference can give you the courage to take on this task, but you'll benefit from support for yourself as well and we will address that shortly.

Here's a few questions to ask yourself to help work out how you're feeling and what you can do:

- On a scale of 1 (*not concerned at all*) to 10 (*extremely concerned*) about the risk of suicide to your teenager right now, how would you rate yourself? Has this changed over the last week, month or year?

- What is it that made you place yourself on the scale where you did? (e.g., warning signs, something your teenager said, a gut feeling).

- If you were to make a small change to act on your concern or reduce your worry what would it be? Be practical and clear about this, remembering that there are many small things you can do (e.g. ask your teenager if they are having thoughts of suicide, remove access to means, organise a family dinner or activity). We will look at more ways to do this in the next section.

- If you review the list of risk and protective factors for suicide which ones jump out at you? What is your response as you identify these (bearing in mind that some of them in isolation are not necessarily related to suicide risk)? Where are the strengths and weaknesses for your teenager? Which of the protective factors can you increase? Which of the risk factors can you do something about?

- Who can you share your current concerns with? Do you have a family member or friend you are comfortable with? Do you have a mental health professional you are in touch with? Would you consider calling a helpline?

Chapter 7

Understanding suicide from a young person's perspective

Finding opportunities to listen to our teenagers will be the only way to actually understand their unique experience in relation to suicidality. That may take some time and it may be helpful to have some idea about the kinds of experiences other young people have reported (or what older people say when looking back on their experiences as a young person who was suicidal). This chapter is necessarily confronting and you may choose to read it now, read it in small sections or come back to it later. There will be times when you want to only focus on the practicalities of supporting your teenager. There may be other times when you crave information about what might be causing the situation your teenager is in. You might be looking for ways to begin the conversation, or you might want to be prepared for what your teenager may tell you.

It's difficult to find information about what is going on in the mind of a person who is suicidal. If we knew, or if it was simply one or two things, we would be clearer about what to do to prevent suicides. We do know that many young people have thoughts of suicide. These may be fleeting and related to a stress or situation that is affecting them at that time. These thoughts may be vague and not really thought through. The thoughts may not necessarily go beyond the thought into a plan. For other young people, the thoughts can be more chronic, occurring every day and not related to one specific situation but a more general hopelessness or feeling that things will never get any better or there's no way out of their current situation. They may have started to explore possibilities for killing themselves which they then develop and refine into an actual plan. This may happen quickly or develop over a long period of time. The way this unfolds can depend on the level of distress the young person experiences. Perhaps the person's temperament may also play a role. They may have an ultimatum in their mind — for example if this happens (or doesn't happen) then I'll go ahead with the plan to die. Perhaps their thought processes become stuck and their focus becomes so narrow they can't see any other way out of their situation. Maybe there is alcohol or other drug use that impacts their thinking as well. Maybe they become influenced by others (known as suicide contagion), which was one of the main concerns about the *13 Reasons Why* series (Netflix, 2017) which gives them the motivation to go ahead. This speculation about all of the various possibilities might not seem helpful but the point is that there are likely many different factors that come together to lead the young person to the decision and towards the act that can lead to their death. Each young person will have their own experience. While this can seem overwhelming and may lead to us feeling helpless, it also means that there are many points at which we can intervene. Small acts of noticing, of being there, ready to listen and finding a way to interrupt or intervene will most certainly make a difference.

When I was looking for information to help us to understand what might be happening at the point a young person is thinking about suicide, I was drawn to reading about suicide notes. If the person who died left a suicide note, we may glean some information about what was going on for them at the time they wrote the note and were planning their death. Not everyone who dies by suicide leaves a suicide note. A recent study in Norway of suicide among young people used a qualitative textual analysis of suicide notes to try to understand the background behind the person's decision to die by suicide (Freuchen, Ulland & Mesel, 2018). They found a tendency for young people to have tunnel vision and singularly obsessed with a specific traumatic experience. Common features of the suicide notes included:

- Description of the intolerable situation the young person faced at the time of the suicide — an overwhelming inner pain related to a situation that was no longer bearable.

- Planning and elaboration was evident. The notes suggested that the death was not the result of a sudden impulse or a sudden strong negative emotion. Rather, the notes revealed situations that had become unbearable over time.

- A number of common themes were identified, including:

    - Declarations of love, affection and friendship — often addressed to parents, siblings and friends.

    - Offers of consolation and forgiveness — acknowledging the loss and grief that would come to the family and friends reading the note. Some notes also attempted to relieve the reader of possible guilt stating that their suicidal act wasn't their fault.

    - Feelings of guilt, shame and aggression — feelings that could not be ameliorated in ways other than by ending their lives. Some notes included specific incidents where the young person felt responsible and guilty or a general description of guilt. Shame was identified in some notes with lists of failures, regrets and burdens. Some of the notes expressed anger directed towards other people, as well as anger directed towards themselves.

    - Closing statements — last will and testament, distribution of belongings and arrangements for the care of pets.

Psychological autopsies conducted by coroners or other legal officials also provide information but this relies upon what people close to the person knew or were willing to share. Historically there's been a lot of secrecy and shame attached to suicide and this means that there can be hesitation about what information is shared. I've mentioned before that young people don't always share their innermost thoughts and feelings, partly because of the nature of adolescent development but also due to shame and fear associated with mental health problems and suicide. Research with young people who are suicidal is also restricted due to ethical considerations so there is still a lot we don't know about young people's experience of suicidality.

Hearing from people who lived after a suicide attempt is another way of gathering information but the focus after a suicide attempt necessarily needs to be on getting help and planning to live safely so sharing the story of their suicidality may be counterproductive. We increasingly are hearing stories from people who have experienced suicide attempts or are bereaved by suicide, called 'lived experiences'. We can't be sure that people who die by suicide have the same experiences as those who attempt suicide and don't die. It is essential however that we try to understand the experience so we can know what it is that matters most. There may be differences between individuals of course but having insight into another's experience can provide us with clues that we might find helpful or at least help us to come closer to a deeper understanding of what it is like.

One of the most useful sources of information I found was the memoir titled *Eight Stories Up. An adolescent chooses hope over suicide*, written by Dequincy A. Lezine, PhD. He wrote the book as a Postdoctoral Research Fellow at the University of Rochester Centre for the Study and Prevention of Suicide. His co-author, David Brent, MD, is an academic specialising in child psychiatry. Dequincy was suicidal as a teenager and when the book was published in 2008, he was 31 years old. After his first-hand experience with suicide, he now works to prevent suicide in adolescents and his memoir serves as his story and a handbook for young people. He's obviously spent a lot of time reflecting on and learning from his own experiences for the benefit of others.

In this section I'll provide some of the insights from Dequincy's book that I think are most relevant for us. In the first chapter of the book, titled 'Crisis', he describes in some detail the situation he found himself in when finalising plans for his suicide as an 18-year old college student. He includes a journal entry written at 4 am:

> I think I flipped today … I talked to Mom on the phone and that question, 'How do you feel?' came up again. How do I feel? Does she really want to know? Frustrated by goal-driven, hopeless yet motivated, alone with friends, lost but in the middle of it all, like I've lost all faith, yet stronger than I've ever been (2008, p. 1).

The entry continues describing his head as feeling like 'a million and 15 different people' were living inside. He also stated that he was doing what he wanted to do yet it wasn't what he had expected to do. In fact he wasn't sure whether he would succeed. He described efforts he'd made to 'keep it together' — visiting people, venting, eating chocolate with a good friend. His friend told him he looked sad, 'like a little kid whose puppy died'. He was hurting but didn't know why.

As the adult reflecting on this time, he describes the multiple events or situations (risk factors) that come together to increase the chances a person will attempt suicide. With the insight of his own experience, he notes the paradox of suicide that despite this complexity it can seem that it happens for a single reason. The risk factors pile up as bad things happen and there is a moment when the person crosses a threshold which tips them closer to suicide risk. He can now see that his suicidal crisis was like a tsunami, beginning with a small ripple before the sea rushed in to engulf his world. Its force meant he couldn't outrun it or hide from it. He described being terrified by it.

He also describes what it was like to cross the threshold from being 'at risk of suicide' to 'suicidal'. He was aware that over the years he had learned to numb himself from stressful situations. For reasons he doesn't explain, he had learned to sweep memories of childhood under his 'mental rug' into a jar, which inevitably broke. As the jar broke, all of the pent-up emotions of his past rushed in to torment him. He lacked the emotional vocabulary to describe them, labelling them instead as anger, a term he now recognises as a 'stereotypical male emotional response'. What he really experienced was an 'unhealthy onslaught of disappointment, anxiety, and shame'.

As I read Dequincy's account, I regularly paused to reflect on his story. Many of us experience such feelings of confusion and doubt and may have learned to hide away feelings from our childhoods. And we may have had times when these feelings spilled over. But not everyone becomes suicidal when this tsunami, as he described it, happens. Surely there's more. And as I read on, yes, there is. He describes feeling alone, feeling like he doesn't fit in, having experienced rejection during his childhood and living his life feeling like he was 'on the fringes', an 'outcast'. Despite his acceptance at university, he still felt like a 'pathetic failure' who was 'absolutely worthless'. He describes his soul as being crushed by despair and feeling burdened by heartache, misery and anguish. He could usually figure things out and took pride in this but during this period of emotional anguish he was confused and frustrated that he couldn't do what he usually did and figure it all out. It was within that context where it seems that his external and internal worlds were colliding that he began to have thoughts that death would be an option. To others he may have looked like things were going well, yet inside himself he was having suicidal thoughts. This is an important point for us as parents to be aware. Checking in, hearing the answers we want to hear, that things are going well, isn't enough. We need to notice, check in with more intent, greater depth, to reach under the surface, really listen to how things are. We need to try to understand whether the external appearance matches how the young person is actually feeling inside. We need to look for small signs that might not match what the young person is saying. Giving our teenagers permission to tell us if it isn't, helping them to locate words, maybe new or unfamiliar words that describe feelings, to let us know that things are not all right. Trusting that they can share this with us and we will be able to handle it. Drawing might help if words fail. Mostly, we need to be ready to listen and let them know that this is something we are ready to hear and want to help them with. Sitting together in silence can give the young person time to process their thoughts and find the words. We might want to consider what things we can let go of for the time being, like the messy bedroom or the unfinished homework, as we recognise that there may well be much bigger things at stake right now.

We also need to let them know that if things are not going as well as planned, or hoped, that this is not a problem and in fact is part of life and it's our job to be there with them, walking beside them, during these times. Dequincy worried about how his family would see his failure. He believed that he was supposed to reward his family for their sacrifices of sending him to college and that he was meant to become a role model for the other children in the family. He recalled how proud the family had been of him when he left for college. He was also worried about what people would think of him if he told them his real feelings. He worried that people would think that he was 'crazy'. All of this came together to make him feel that no-one could understand how he felt, further isolating him from seeking help and adding to the burden where he could see the only solution was to die. There's a certain irony about the burden of family pride for parents. While we want to show our kids how proud we are of them, it can be a weight on their shoulders.

Dequincy shared how death became a particular focus for him as suicidal thoughts increased and became difficult to shake off. He described the suicidal urge as becoming a 'constant and unwanted companion, slowly but surely wearing down' his will to live. Death became seen by him as the only way to relieve his distress and to give him peace. This is significant to notice — death by suicide was about relieving the pain of living and the only way he could see to rid himself of the negative emotions and thoughts which were ruling his mind. He also described his interest in finding a way that would help his family and friends understand how desperate and painful his life had become. This suggests that suicidal behaviour can be a way of communicating extreme emotions and thoughts that don't easily have words for sharing. It can also seem like the obvious solution to problems as other options narrow down and the ability to problem solve is reduced.

Dequincy's story reveals how young people can be active in seeking help or changing their circumstances. He sought out help through web sites. This helped him in two ways: to recognise that he was in danger and to feel less alone. These internet searches were helpful but also dangerous as they gave him actual information or instructions about ways to die, particularly which methods were likely to be fatal. Ambivalence was at play at the same time as he was exploring and testing out ways to die, he was also aware that part of him didn't want to go through with it. He is clear that he wanted to get rid of the pain most of all and he became stuck with the idea of dying as the only way to do that. This is significant and common in stories from people who express suicidal thoughts and intents, along with relief when the person attempting suicide didn't actually die or seriously injure themselves. This ambivalence is key to us being able to help our kids as it provides an opportunity to find ways to help.

Knowing where to begin to get help can be difficult and Dequincy provides some insights into this. He talks about two ways that young people can move away from the suicidal crisis and 'tip the scales in favour of life':

1. Solve the problems to decrease the reasons for dying, and

2. Live a happy and meaningful life to increase the reasons for living.

Focusing on both of these at the same time can mean that parents can find more than one way to begin to help. Taking small steps to promote enjoyment can be helpful, just as finding ways to deal with the overwhelming feelings will be. Searching for ways to promote hope and a sense of control while removing as many means as possible (including medications and weapons) may provide a focus. Dequincy did note that he was glad he didn't have access to alcohol or drugs or it may have impacted on his ability to think through his decisions. His description of his experience also suggests that his temperament wasn't an impulsive one. He liked to think through things, to take time to slowly plan and make decisions. This was no doubt protective for him.

Dequincy describes what he calls 'passive' attempts to die: risky behaviours that might lead to his death rather than more self-directed efforts. This fits with the ambivalence he was feeling and recognises that acting upon the desire to die can be a difficult thing to do. This helps us to learn that we must take notice of our teenager's behaviour. For younger teenagers this may mean increasing supervision and time with them. For older teenagers it may not be so easy to monitor but we can ask them about how they are spending their time, what their plans are for the day or evening and encourage them to spend time with you or others.

Dequincy helps us to gain a sense of what it might take to move from initial thoughts to suicidal planning and then towards the decision to act on the plan. He describes being rejected by a girl he liked. He then proceeded to spend the night and next day writing emails to explain his plan to die, describing a feeling of nothingness and asking people to give up on him. He later described this as like the calm before the storm, like he had finally found a sensation of peace because the decision to die had been made. He had written a suicide note and knew what he was planning to do but still described the battle in his mind as part of his brain wanted him to die and the other part wanted him to survive. In effect this reaching out by email ended up saving his life because his friends kept him talking while also contacting police to ask them to go to his room at the university. This highlights the importance of everyone taking talk of suicide seriously and acting to ensure that the young person is kept alive.

In describing the 'background story' Dequincy acknowledges the difficulties in revisiting his past, even when writing the book to provide context for the suicidal crisis. He notes that along with the negative parts of his life he had also not thought about the positive times he had. He believed that was because he became so focused on the negative and removing all thoughts and feelings from the past that the positive was obliterated as well. This gives us another pointer, another way of helping our teenagers to keep a perspective, to regain a balance that comes from allowing the positives to shine through, without ignoring or dismissing the power of the negatives. Young people will need to know that we understand the depth of their feelings, even when we are encouraging them to embrace the positive experiences and strengths and capacities they have. As parents, we might not always know about the negatives.

Dequincy describes the ways that he tried to drop hints to people about how bad he was feeling — through the music he played with lyrics of depression, anger, loneliness, and suicide. He wrote a piece of music titled *Young Suicide* and he changed the way he dressed, wearing a hood and shading his eyes. He avoided people and withdrew from social situations. He acknowledges that he also gave off mixed messages, sometimes smiling and laughing, still visiting friends. He took pride in finding ways to hide his heartache. He didn't share openly his feelings until finally some friends noticed and asked him about it. For a long time, however, he says that nobody asked. Keeping the lines of communication open sounds simple and we probably think we are doing it but it's clear from Dequincy's story that we can't just rely on verbal word exchanges. It also requires us to notice the smallest of changes and vigilantly remaining curious. Asking explicitly if they feel suicidal might be the opening the young person needs to be able to share the depth of feelings they have. Remember that they won't get the idea of suicide from us asking about it. If they are feeling suicidal and we ask it might just be the door you are looking for that opens up the opportunity to learn how they are feeling and then to be able to help them. They may feel relieved that it is acceptable to talk about and that there's no need to hide from it. If they're not feeling suicidal they can say that but they will know that we're prepared to talk about it if they want to.

Reflection: Understanding suicide from a young person's perspective

- What stands out for you after reading this section?

- What hadn't you thought about before?

- What surprised you?

- What sounded familiar?

- What do you think about the idea of growth beyond a suicide attempt? Do you think there will be opportunities for you all to learn and grow from this experience now or later on?

- Are there ideas you can take for yourself and act upon now?

Chapter 8

The experience of being a parent of a teenager who is suicidal

There has been some research that can help us to understand the experiences of parents who have had a teenager who was suicidal. A study conducted in 2012 in Denmark explored the experiences of parents who teenagers attempted suicide (Buus, Caspersen, Hansen, Stenager, & Fleischer, 2014). Although it was a small study of 14 parents who had attended a counselling service after their teenagers had attempted suicide, it provides important insights that I expect will resonate with parents going through this experience. The themes that came through that research is consistent with what has been reported in other research. This section will likely be challenging reading and it might help to take your time or have someone to talk to about it as you read it. Understanding what normal reactions might be to such a situation can help us to make sense of our own feelings and not feel so alone.

Parents in the studies sometimes described their experiences of parenting a suicidal teenager as a 'double trauma' — the trauma of the suicide attempt(s) and the accompanying impact on the family's well being. Researchers found that:

> [T]he family experiences their child's first suicide attempt in a way resembling the youth's experience: loss of hope, blame, guilt, self-recrimination, a sense of total failure, rejection, isolation and incomprehension; powerlessness and helplessness, loss of control. (Buus et al., 2014, p. 829)

Others found that suicidal acts were sometimes seen by parents as a rejection of them, based on their child's attempt to reject life. This feeling of not being wanted by their child and recognising that dying was more attractive than living for their child at the point of suicide attempt led to considerable distress in parents. For some mothers, the feelings of rejection and despair were so strong that they sometimes felt that life would be easier if the child died or if they died themselves before their child did.

The research highlights that the period leading up to the suicide attempt can vary — for many of the families the suicide attempt was the culmination of a prolonged period, sometimes of several years, where their teenager experienced psychological problems and their behaviour was of concern (including self-harm and eating disorders). Efforts to obtain satisfactory help had been unsuccessful and parents had become powerless in responding effectively to their teenagers' escalating situation. Some young people had received mental health diagnoses and treatment, while others hadn't. Parents searched for explanations and blamed negative family events, such as death, illness and family breakdowns for their adolescent's struggles. For some parents, this first suicide attempt after such a prolonged struggle had felt like a relief as they'd feared it for such a long time and they hoped that hitting 'rock bottom' might mean they could enact some change in getting help. For a minority of parents in the study, the suicide attempt had come out of the blue without prior warning. For those parents, they learned for the first time of the degree of distress and level of severity of their teenager's problems.

The experience of being a parent of a young person who has attempted suicide is often described in dramatic ways that reflect the extent of distress and trauma associated with both knowing how desperate the teenager is feeling as well as the confusion and desperate struggle to find help. Some parents in the studies physically found their child after the suicide attempt whereas other parents received news about the attempt from others, including emergency health staff. What followed for all of them was a period of emotional distress and physical intervening to keep the young person safe. For many parents, this meant being in a constant state of distress and alarm, including standing guard or sleeping outside of the teenager's door, or following young people who ran away. Once the situation stabilised, the parents reported still feeling triggered by reminders of the suicide attempt with accompanying fears flooding back. The sound of incoming text messages and phone calls was one of the most common triggers as this reminded them of the catastrophic news they'd received previously. Long periods of continual ruminations often accompanied even the stable periods as parents worried that periods of calm may not last as they faced the possible death of their child. This led to changes in parenting, with some parents becoming more lenient and others overreacting. Parents sometimes felt a need to constantly check on the safety and whereabouts of their children, causing a hypervigilance. Such hypervigilance then led to a lack of any relaxed time or ability to concentrate on other things for the mothers, including working, eating and sleeping.

All parents reported their desperate efforts to support their teenager after the suicide attempt. Despite their best efforts, they often felt futile and powerless. There were often discouraging setbacks, when suicidal behaviour occurred again, hopes were dashed or promises were broken. Strong feelings of intense hate and blame sometimes arose alongside the feelings of worry and hopelessness, particularly when the family's wellbeing was threatened by the teenagers' behaviours. The psychological pressure on the family was often reported to be intense, partly due to the unpredictable character of suicide attempts. For some parents this resulted in feelings of wanting to give up on their teenagers as they faced an uncertain future that they believed would continue to involve suicide attempts. Some of the participants in the study reported their own suicidal thoughts as the pressure became unbearable and prolonged.

Parents reported feeling guilty after their teenager's first suicide attempt, because they felt responsible for bringing them up:

> It was me, who brought her into the world, me who formed her and it was me who let her down and it was more or less my fault that she got so far out as to trying suicide. (Buus et al., 2014, p. 828).

Mothers described a sense of failure, speaking at length about blame, self-recrimination and a sense of total failure. Being an inadequate parent was also associated with parents attributing blame to themselves when their adolescents had mental health disorders, with a belief that they had not been sufficiently devoted, self-sacrificing and attentive to their child. This also related to a feeling of horror at missing the warning signs and not responding earlier to their child's distress. This led to a doubting and distrust in their parenting skills, which in turn led to insecurity across other spheres of their lives and interactions. It also sometimes led to an attempt to become the perfect mother, who never made mistakes or missed vital clues in the future.

The sense of failure in their parenting role led to feelings of shame and isolation as parents felt too uncomfortable to share their story with others. The shame related to their teenager's behaviour, their inability to stop the behaviour despite their many efforts and the belief that there must be something wrong with the family for this behaviour to occur.

The relationship between the parents and teenagers inevitably changed as a result of the suicidal behaviour. Parents became hypervigilant and attentive as they tried to stop another suicide attempt. Many of the parents in the study spoke about how the focus on keeping their teenager alive meant that they lost confidence in their typical parenting approaches and their values were undermined as they gave their teenager special privileges:

> Suddenly the foundation you have built on crumbles, because you always go round with a guilty conscience about doing something wrong. And suddenly you begin to be a pleaser, because you are frightened out of your wits. (Buus et al., 2014, p. 828)

Pressure on other family members was often substantial and even when parents are in long-term relationships family arguments and conflicts placed pressure on the family, with concerns that divorce might become a possibility. Each parent had a different relationship with the young person. The young person would sometimes tell one parent something they didn't share with the other and this was sometimes experienced by the parents as being 'played off' against each other. A further complication and source of stress was the different ways of managing the situation by each parent. Sometimes this meant that one parent felt disloyal to the other by the way they were trying to help the teenager, sometimes disregarding agreements that had been made previously in efforts to handle the situation as best as they could. Some parents reported this changing over time, perhaps beginning with agreement at the start when there was an explicit focus on keeping the teenager alive:

> We really stuck together, there were no problems. A vacuum develops afterwards, where you realise that it's perhaps difficult to keep your balance right there. 'Who did what? 'Did you say something wrong or?' 'I don't think you should have done that.' 'You shouldn't have let her go to that party', or something or other. (Buus et al., 2014, p. 829)

One participant noted that all families have conflicts so this situation might not be unusual, however, the stakes were higher when a family member was suicidal: 'There's just the unique difference that the consequences can be fatal, if you make a wrong decision' (Buus et al., 2014, p. 829).

The impact on siblings varied, with some siblings being very protective toward the teenager who was suicidal, whereas in other families the siblings felt neglected because of the extra attention paid to the teenager. This sometimes led to siblings saying they hated the teenager who was suicidal and avoided connections with them. In other families, the participants believed that some of the problems and illnesses experienced by the siblings had been caused by the damaged family dynamics and their needs being neglected.

Parents reported feeling severely emotionally and socially traumatised by their teenager's suicide attempt, feelings of disempowerment and the extensive impact on the family's interpersonal relationships. The parents described attempts to manage societal reactions and efforts to repair the disruption to the family's life. This impacted on their identity as parents and the need to be seen as morally adequate and responsible parents who shouldn't be held responsible for their teenager's unhappiness and behaviour. Although some of the pressures were similar to those of parents of children with life-threatening behaviours who faced care-giving stress and fears about death of their child, the participants of teenagers who were suicidal experience much more guilt because they regarded themselves as being responsible for their teenager's situation. There was also greater shame associated with the teenager who was suicidal compared to a child with a physical health condition.

Feelings of helplessness arose from many sources, including the extent to which the young person's behaviour had taken over the focus of the family's life, placing great strain on family members and impacting on the relationships between the parents and each of their children. While mothers ruminated over ways to stop further suicide attempts, these efforts sometimes proved to be in vain, leading to a sense of greater helplessness as their actions brought no positive change in circumstances. This helplessness as a parent to make their child better was particularly poignant for some mothers who compared it to their role as a parent of a younger child when they were more easily able to tend to their child's hurt. Suicide attempts provided an unfamiliar and distressing circumstance for parents when their past parenting or life experiences did not equip them with knowledge and skills to help them to cope.

The extent to which the young person's behaviour had taken over the focus of the family's life led to feelings of helplessness for parents and placed strains on family members which impacted on the relationships between the parents and each of their children. Efforts to prevent further suicide attempts were sometimes unsuccessful, which led to a greater sense of helplessness as a parent in caring protectively for their child.

Described by one mother as feeling like a steel drum with nothing in it, mothers reported feeling alone with their worries about their child even when they knew that others were concerned. This sometimes related to a lack of sensitivity and understanding from other parents or family members, who expressed views that the child might be seeking attention, for example. The sense of isolation also related to the mothers' relationship with their spouses as they sometimes struggled to express their feelings and believed that the fathers could not experience the same feelings as they did. This led to deterioration in marriages as the mothers devoted more time to their child and had little energy to maintain or repair the spousal relationship.

The isolation was also felt in relation to extended family members and even health professionals, who sometimes expressed a lack of understanding or anger towards the adolescent. The mothers also reported a stigma associated with the suicidal behaviour, leading to a silencing and sense of it being a taboo topic. Of great significance in terms of receiving support, the mothers reported that their children's behaviour created a chasm between them and their friends who were also parenting teenagers, as their day to day stressors became further removed from what were seen to be more normal worries that other parents faced.

One mother described the uneasiness and hesitation which came with her parenting after her child's suicidal attempts as having a monkey on her back, clinging on and clawing onto her. This prevented her from ever feeling like she was at rest. The mothers reported being fearful of saying the wrong thing or acting in a way which could trigger the next suicide attempt and this meant they became very cautious in their interactions with their adolescent, avoiding confrontation, often described as walking on eggshells.

Parents reported a negative change in their relationships with their children since the onset of the suicidal behaviours with an emotional distance occurring due to the lack of trust and having been burned emotionally too many times before, alongside a lack of ability to comprehend what is happening. The emotional distance could have been a form of self-defence to distance themselves from what is frightening, or even preparation for, the possibility of their child's death.

One of the sources of support highlighted in the research was the meeting of other parents in similar situations with whom parents could share their feelings of shame and embarrassment. With the support of a counsellor they were able to create a space for mutual support to share and discuss ways of managing their situations, to voice what they considered to be socially illegitimate feelings and to confess what they felt were wrongdoings with each other.

Parenting a teenager who is suicidal

Chapter 9

Safety first — managing the suicidal crisis

When your teenager is suicidal the main priority is their safety. This means taking what they say seriously. If they share suicidal thoughts, it's important to find out whether they have a plan to act on these feelings. Remember that suicidal thoughts are common and don't mean necessarily that the person is going to act on them. This will be quite different to a situation where they have actually tried to harm themselves because they wanted to die. The way we respond to keep them safe will vary depending on what is happening and what they are planning to do. Remember that they may not always share all of their plans with us. Being prepared to listen without judgement will help them feel more comfortable to talk honestly about how they are feeling and any plans they have. Having others available to talk with them will be important. Letting them know that we are happy for them to talk to others will give them the freedom to talk to people they trust who may be able to help. This is the time to open the door to a range of supports, not feel like we are the only ones that can help. Remember too that young people want to be independent and make their own choices so anything we do that undermines that will be likely to push them away and risk silencing them.

What might a crisis look like?

If your teenager has harmed themselves it will be obvious that you need to seek immediate emergency help, however, if you become aware that the situation is escalating you may not be sure what to look for. It is important to understand the methods of suicide used by young people. These methods include overdosing on over-the-counter, prescription, and non-prescription medicine, cutting with a range of implements, including knives and blades, hanging using ropes or belts, jumping from heights, being run over by trains or cars or guns or other weapons. We know from the statistics that males are more likely to die from suicide and use more lethal methods than females, although females attempt suicide more often. Looking out for the stockpiling of medications or gathering of items that could be used to hurt themselves, and identifying and removing these, is an effective suicide prevention strategy.

Seeking immediate help during a crisis

There are a number of possibilities for seeking help. The most useful ones will depend on what is actually happening at the time. The following table teases out the types of behaviours and concerns you may have and includes a list of options for you and your teenager to seek help for each one. It's important to neither overreact nor underreact — and that's not always easy to judge. In an emergency call 000. If the young person is in no immediate danger, call a helpline service and talk through your concerns to gain some perspective on the situation, or use online resources for further information (see Table 9.1).

If you are in a situation where your teenager is actively suicidal, it is essential that you focus on safety first. This may require calling an ambulance who may also call the police to attend. This can be extremely confronting for you and your teenager and some people worry about the public display this creates. If you believe it is safe enough to do so you might choose to take your teenager to the emergency department of your hospital yourself. Bear in mind that you may be feeling distressed and driving may

Table 9.1 Emergency and other resources for concerning behaviours

Concern	Behaviour	How to help
Serious concerns and emergency help is required	• Young person has attempted suicide/injured themselves or taken substances with the intention of dying	• Call 000 and ask for an ambulance (note that the police may also attend if there are any concerns about the young person's behaviour); or
		• If safe to do so, take the young person to the local hospital emergency department (only consider this if you are able to do so safely, and the young person is willing to go).
		• As far as possible, remove means of suicide.
	• Young person is very distressed and you are concerned about their safety or the safety of others; or	• Call 000 and ask for an ambulance (note that the police may also attend if there are any concerns about the young person's behaviour); or
	• Young person is talking about suicide and threatening to do something to harm themselves in the immediate future.	• If safe to do so, take the young person to the local hospital emergency department (only if you are able to do this safely and the young person is willing to go).
		• As far as possible, remove means of suicide.
	• Young person is talking about suicide and may be distressed, but is not actively suicidal (i.e., not talking about an immediate plan or behaving in an unsafe way) and the young person is willing to stay with you or another adult.	• Encourage the young person to contact one of the following services or ask if they're happy for you to call for advice. As far as possible provide them with choices:
		- Call the Suicide Call Back Service — 1300 659 467 for young people aged 15 years and over or online chat: www.suicidecallbackservice.org.au
		- Call Kids Helpline 1800 55 1800 or online support for children and young people aged 5 to 25 years: www.kidshelpline.com.au
		- Call Lifeline — 13 11 14 www.lifeline.org.au
		• As far as possible, remove means of suicide.

Table 9.1 continued over page ...

Table 9.1 ... continued

| Concerning behaviour and help will be required | • Young person has made vague comments about suicide but says they have no current plan to kill themselves; and/ or

• Young person's behaviour and mood has changed significantly. You may or may not know what has led to this; and/or

• Young person has been or is likely to be affected by the death by suicide of a friend or other person they knew or felt a strong connection to (bearing in mind that this can be a celebrity or other person they don't have an actual physical connection with). | • Online resources:

- Headspace Centres: www.headspace.org.au

- Reachout: www.reachout.org.au

- Seek out a private psychologist through the Australian Psychological Society's Find a Psychologist web site: www.findapsychologist.org.au

- Seek out the mental health services contact point for your state/territory: https://www.healthdirect.gov.au/australian-health-services

- Review the Head to Health Government web site to see if there are online programs or information that might be helpful: www.headtohealth.gov.au.

• Other resources:

- Previous paediatricians or mental health professionals your teenager has seen.

- Talk to your teenager about asking the family's GP about options for a referral to a mental health professional in your local area.

- Talk to your young person about speaking to a student wellbeing staff member (or other school staff member the young person trusts) about support available at the school and/or in the community.

• As far as possible, remove means of suicide. |

Table 9.1 continued over page ...

Table 9.1 ... continued

Parent is concerned about the young person	• There's no immediate obvious behaviour of concern by the young person and the young person is reluctant to seek help.	• Go to www.parents.au.reachout.com and search for:
		- Information about parenting teenagers
		- Telephone help lines for parents in each state or territory
		- Parents coaching — online one-to-one coaching for parents of teenagers aged 12 — 18 years
		- Online peer support through parents' forum
		- Quiz to help you identify the type of help that is the best fit for you.
		• Talk to your GP about options for accessing support in your local area. This may include individual counselling or parenting groups.
		• Australian Psychological Society Find a Psychologist www.findapsychologist.org.au
		• Self-help resources on www.headtohealth.gov.au
		• As far as possible, remove means of suicide.

be unsafe. If your teenager's behaviour is unpredictable you may become distracted. You will also need to consider how far away the hospital is and how your teenager will be feeling during the trip. If you have any doubts about driving to the hospital you will be best to call the ambulance.

You will also need to handle how you tell your teenager that you are calling the ambulance. Remember that the goal is to keep your teenager safe firstly and secondly to open the door to getting help. These are distinct things. You may get your teenager to the hospital and he or she may assure the staff that they are safe but if they are suicidal they and you will need some additional help. All of this is easier if you have a plan beforehand. If you know what to expect from the hospital you will be able to make a better decision about getting to the hospital. If the hospital has a mental health staff available, your teenager is more likely to have a comprehensive assessment to explore the factors that are causing him or her to feel suicidal. If the hospital doesn't have this set up there are a range of hospital staff who may see your teenager and the level of assessment and support may vary. Some hospitals may link your teenager into community supports or provide some follow up beyond the time at the hospital, whereas others might not have these links. One of the things you can do is to advocate for support for your teenager.

Types of help available

Emergency departments

Emergency departments are often a first point of call when a young person is actively suicidal but vary in their capacity to respond. Some may be equipped with a mental health crisis team who will be able to undertake a risk assessment fairly promptly, whereas others may not have this onsite and may need to wait for a mental health professional or crisis assessment and treatment team (CATT) to attend. This can take time and may lead to the young person becoming more agitated, particularly as hospitals are not well set up to deal with mental health crises.

Mental health treatment plans from a general practitioner

If the situation is not immediately critical, a mental health treatment plan to see a psychologist might be the best approach to get support. These provide Medicare funded sessions with a psychologist who is registered to provide the service. This will usually occur in private practice, although mental health treatment plans are also often required for accessing Headspace centres as well. The GP will need to gather sufficient information to warrant developing the plan as there are guidelines. This will take longer than a short session so make sure that a longer session is booked when making the appointment. Bear in mind also that some GPs have specific mental health training and also in working with young people while others don't have this. Again when making the appointment it would be useful to ask for the most suitable doctor if possible. To help the doctor with the process of decision making in relation to the appropriateness of the plan and completing the document, it will be helpful to make a list with your teenager of some of their recent symptoms, including:

- Suicidal thoughts (current as well as previous, and when these occur)

- Suicidal or self-harming behaviours (acts of hurting him or herself), including any previous behaviours related to suicide or attempts of suicide

- Sleeping patterns — any changes

- Eating habits — any changes

- Feelings of anxiety

- Feelings of distress or upset

- Feelings of sadness

- Outbursts of anger or aggression

- Physical symptoms (e.g., nausea, dizziness)

- Alcohol and other drug use

- Recent situations that have caused upset (e.g., friendships/relationships difficulties, loss of anyone the young person knows to suicide, other losses, changes in family situations or stressors, changes at school).

Bear in mind of course that your teenager may not feel comfortable sharing all of this with you but it will help for them to have thought it through first and therefore prepared if the doctor asks these questions. For younger teenagers you may be keen to attend the appointment but if they are reluctant to have you there or for older teenagers offer to wait outside. Remember that getting professional help is what is most important and any efforts to intervene that may impact negatively on that will be unhelpful. Your teenager will be more likely to take responsibility for their own mental health and safety if we give them this space.

Hospitalisation

It is not common for young people to be hospitalised due to suicidality, although following a suicide attempt a young person may remain in hospital for a period of time for monitoring, treatment of physical injuries if there are any and while a plan is developed for them to be able to leave safely. There are some inpatient services for young people experiencing difficulties with their mental health but these are not readily available and their suitability will depend upon the needs of your teenager and the target group for the inpatient service.

While hospitalisation may help you to feel more secure in relation to your teenager's safety, bear in mind that there are risks associated with hospitalisation and it would only ever be for a short period of time unless there are serious mental health issues that need to be managed. When a young person leaves a hospital they can be at an increased risk of suicide and will need careful monitoring with the safety plan and follow up appointments. It will be important for you to ask at the hospital what these arrangements are and what role you should play.

Technology

There are now a range of mental health apps and programs available online that are currently being researched. They may not necessarily be targeted to what your teenager will need when they are suicidal. It will therefore be best to talk to mental health professionals about the best approach to supporting your teenager and whether any apps or online programs would be helpful.

You may like to take some time to identify local services in your area now so you have these handy in the event that you require them. There will be differences across regions and some services will be more easily accessed than others.

- Local GP phone number
- Emergency hospital phone number
- Local mental health professional
- Public mental health service (including CATT)
- Local child and adolescent mental health service
- Local Headspace.

In an ideal world, you will be able to seek help and access it quickly getting the kind of support that is going to work immediately for your teenager. In the real world, however, we are still working towards a system that enables this to occur. In some geographical locations there are programs that are being trialled and may be helpful.

In regional or remote communities, there will be less options and services may be overcommitted. Seeing your role as a support and an advocate for your teenager will be important in any of these situations. While I don't want to send a message of hopelessness, I want you to be prepared for the challenges that can be involved in getting help, are aware of as many options as possible and ensure that you feel confident to keep asking for help, asking questions that will prompt the best support possible and importantly never give up on accessing help.

At a bare minimum, contacting a telephone or online help centre and encouraging your teenager to do this can keep you connected to others. Don't allow yourselves to become isolated and show your teenager that you are there for the long haul and that together you will get through the difficult times. Trust that your presence and your commitment to your teenager will give them courage and support that can be life-preserving.

Assessments

A comprehensive psychosocial assessment that focuses on all the facets of the young person's life (and not just the suicidal thoughts and behaviours in isolation) is required to help to identify the level of need a young person has when experiencing suicidal thoughts or showing signs of suicidal behaviour. There's been much debate about how a suicide risk assessment should be undertaken and how reliable and effective they are in predicting suicide in the near or distant future. In fact it's been known for decades that suicide risk assessment tools alone are not reliable in helping to determine actual risk. This can be related to a number of reasons, perhaps because people who are experiencing suicidal thoughts or plans may not be clear about what their feelings and intentions are, may not share these with the person undertaking the assessment and even that things change quickly when people are distressed. It's therefore a challenging area and one that mental health professionals take very seriously.

You may be wondering why an assessment takes time or requires the gathering of a lot of information and this is the reason why. The more accurate information that is obtained, the better position the health professional will be in to make an informed decision about the next steps required to support your teenager and to keep them safe.

There are some features that are recognised as important in gathering this information to determine what the young person's needs are. You can support the process by being available to provide information if required and also by explaining to your teenager that this is likely to occur. The better prepared you both are the smoother the process will be. Some of the considerations for the mental health professional undertaking an assessment include:

- A trusting relationship needs to be built quickly for a young person to share how they are feeling and what is going on for them.

- Building in a safety plan as information is gathered during the assessment will help to make sense of the information and ensure the plan is tailored to the individual.

- Understanding the drivers of suicide, through questions that identify what is the most pressing matter that has led to the current situation.

- Recognising the warning signs that add weight to the risk is essential (e.g., previous suicide attempts) but not sufficient to determine the current level of need

- Listening to what the young person believes will help them most at that time.

- Hearing about past experiences will help gain a full picture of what's happening and particularly identify any previous risky behaviours, self-harm or suicide attempts.

- Obtaining information from family members and others can help to gain a better understanding of what is happening.

- Building in supports from family members and other adults as well as friends is essential to reducing risk of suicide.

- Balancing the inclusion of family members with the confidentiality of the young person's information. If the young person does not feel confident that their information will be kept confidential they may not share openly. Parents can support this process by being available but also focusing on what they can do that will be helpful.

Chapter 10

Safety planning

O nce you become aware that your teenager is experiencing suicidal thoughts or has attempted suicide you will immediately want to help them get some support. This can take time and knowing where to begin can be the first challenge. There are a few different scenarios to consider. If this is the first time concerns have been raised, it will be quite different to a situation where your teenager has felt or behaved this way before. If your teenager is already seeing a mental health professional you will have a starting point. If he or she did attempt suicide they may already be at the emergency department of a hospital, hopefully accessing a mental health risk assessment. At least in each of these situations there will be mental health professionals who are aware of the situation.

However, if neither of those situations apply you will find yourself trying to work out what to do and who can help. Your teenager may or may not be willing to seek help and the reality is that we can't make them see someone. If you believe that your teenager is imminently at risk, you will want to seek help from emergency services. It's important to remember that even if you call an ambulance or the Crisis Assessment and Treatment Team (CATT), they can only help as much as your teenager is willing to let them. If they don't feel that there is an immediate risk they may not take the teenager with them but will leave them with you. Remember that hospitalisation for suicidality doesn't offer a long-term solution and in fact may increase the risk of suicide.

It can be helpful to remember that your teenager may be feeling over-whelmed and out of control. This may mean that they gain comfort from you taking control and getting them help or it can mean the opposite, that they want to withdraw and not talk about how they are feeling or what they are planning with you or anyone else. You know your teenager well so you can be the best person to judge this, although bear in mind that you might be entering new territory now. You may feel like your teenager is more like a stranger and you can no longer predict their behaviour. You might be able to think through the typical ways your teenager behaves and what has worked in the past when they have been stressed. Thinking about this might also help you plan how to approach your teenager. You might ask them what will help them, for example, rather than making the decision yourself. The older they are the more important this will be, remembering the drive to independence that we've looked at previously. For anyone who is actively suicidal however, regardless of age, we need to be more assertive and make it clear that we need to get some help. Planning how the help will happen can be the focus and including them in decisions, by giving them a couple of choices if they can't come up with ideas for themselves, can be helpful.

Bear in mind also that not everyone knows how to ask to help. Depending upon your teenager's age and stage of independence, there are a couple of options. Your teenager may be happy for you to make the initial phone call. Encourage them to sit with you so they hear what is being said. You might use the loud speaker function on the phone so that they are included. Be ready to hand over the conversation to the young person as quickly as possible. This will help them to gain a sense of control and feel like people are listening to them. If they want to make a phone call them-selves you could help them by practicing what they will say. You might write down some dot points together as a prompt. Some of the information you could be asked when seeking help is listed below. There will be some of these questions that seem irrelevant to the current circumstances and can be frustrating to have to answer but it's useful to remember that the person taking your information has phone calls from many people with a wide range of circumstances. They will be able to make the best decision about how or who can help by getting as much information as possible. This can take time and being prepared with as much information as possible but also prepared for the time it can take will help to reduce frustration. Keeping a focus on hopefulness can be difficult when seeking help in the first instance but will be critical to prevent your young person's risk increasing.

Working through this list together might help you also to identify what kind of support you need. You could use the phone numbers and web sites in the Introduction to come up with a list of organisations or people to contact:

- *Basic information such as age, gender and place of residence.* Organisations often have criteria related to funding that can restrict who they can see; health professionals also have particular skill sets (e.g., not all of them work with adolescents).

- *The most pressing problem.* Describe current feelings and behaviours and particularly safety risks. If suicidal thoughts or behaviours are present, and a suicide risk assessment hasn't been completed, this should be the priority and this will help you to work out where to start. It may be that a phone call to the emergency department of hospitals in your surrounding area can help you to decide where to start. It is better for the emergency department to know that you are on the way rather than turn up and wait if there is no one there to conduct the risk assessment. While some waiting can be expected, sitting in a hospital waiting room for a long time can add to the feelings of agitation and helplessness.

- *What do you need right now?* This is important if there is a safety risk. Not all services or professionals can provide sufficient support if the risk is high.

- *Have you ever accessed mental health support before? If so, when and who?* This might serve as a discussion point about re-connecting with a previous service or reasons why this would not be appropriate or possible at the moment.

- *Do you have a current mental health care plan from the general practitioner?* This will be important for private practitioners as it will enable your teenager to be seen with costs covered by Medicare. Not all practitioners bulk bill so there may be an additional charge. The mental health care plan is developed by the GP. The GP can be a good first point of contact for this reason. It can be better to have a GP that knows your teenager and family well to complete the Plan but in reality it is possible that your family doesn't have one GP or the time when you need the Plan to be completed will be when your GP is not available. Finding a regular GP who has an interest and has undertaken additional training in mental health can be helpful. Some GPs also have a special interest and have done training in working with young people. Seeking these people can mean that your teenager is more likely to feel comfortable attending regularly that may be needed for some time to monitor their mental health even once this crisis passes.

- *Do you have private health extras cover that includes psychology?* This can open additional doors in private health settings and help to cover costs without a mental health care plan.

- *Is the young person using drugs and alcohol?* This may be an important question because some services will want to refer a young person who is using substances to a specific drug and alcohol counselling service. This needs to be considered as part of the overall suicide risk assessment plan.

- *Who does the young person live with? What supports are at home?* This is important because a young person who is homeless or at risk of homelessness will have considerable other needs that will also need to be prioritised.

Increasingly there are telephone hotlines and internet-based services that can be helpful and may be more attractive to your teenager than seeing someone face to face. The important thing is to find options that provide your teenager with the opportunity to make the decision about who will be able to help them. Bear in mind that your teenager can make their own decisions about seeking help, particularly if they are of an age (usually around 14 years) where the health professional determines that they can provide informed consent.

If they do see a health professional, the information they share will be confidential unless they agree that it can be shared with you. As a parent this may feel like you are being excluded from the process, however, it is critical that young people seeking help feel that they can trust the person they see and this means not telling parents everything. Health professionals are bound by confidentiality ethical obligations and this is taken very seriously because they know that developing a trusting relationship with the teenager is necessary in order for any treatment to be effective. If you understand this you will be better equipped to encourage your teenager to see someone. You can talk to your teenager about your understanding of these rules but also be clear that you want to know how best to help as well. Health professionals will be aware of the important role that parents play and may talk with your teenager about what information can be shared with you or whether you can attend parts of the sessions.

If a safety plan is developed that includes you, it is necessary that you are aware of what the plan is and know what to do if necessary. This information is very different to knowing everything that your teenager is talking about in the sessions. It can help to recognise that your teenager seeking help and sharing their thoughts and feelings with a health professional is a big step that you want to support rather than threaten in any way. You can feel confident that the health professional is required to alert you (and others if necessary) if they are concerned about immediate risks related to the teenager. Learning to trust that other adults can help your teenager and appreciating their efforts will set the scene for you to play your parenting role more effectively.

Safety planning and your role

Safety planning is now considered an essential tool for helping a young person and their family and friends to get through difficult times of suicidality. The safety plan should be developed with the young person and should be shared with those people who form part of the support around the young person, such as family members and friends. The safety plan is not the same as a contract. In the past people at risk of suicide were asked to sign a 'no-suicide contract' where they agreed not to do anything that would harm themselves. Such contracts have been found to be not effective for many people, partly because the circumstances can change quickly after signing the contract and the contract itself did little to support the person. The safety plan instead provides a much more useful tool for people that is tailored to their own situation with plans to reduce access to means and listing ideas for coping, including phone numbers and helplines. The plan should be reviewed regularly to include new information or ideas over time.

Some of the questions you may use to start a discussion with the mental health professional and your teenager are:

- What should I look out for (e.g., warning signs/triggers should be outlined in the safety plan)?

- How can I be most helpful?

- Should I ask my teenager if they are okay or should I wait for him or her to come to me?

- What should I do if I am worried about my teenager?

- Who is available to help me if I am worried?

- How can I encourage my teenager to use the safety plan?

- What if my teenager says the safety plan isn't helping?

- If my teenager says he or she is okay but I'm not sure what should I do?

A mental health professional will work with the young person to develop the safety plan to be as comprehensive and useful as possible. This requires the young person to become more aware and able to verbalise those times when they feel suicidal. This can take time and parents may be able to play a helpful role in reporting what they have noticed. The safety plan can help the young person gain a heightened sense of awareness and control over their suicidal thoughts and feelings that accompany (or lead to) those feelings. The plan identifies the triggers that might lead to suicidal thoughts and feelings and ways of coping at that time. An important element of the safety plan is the removal of means of suicide. This is critical as research has shown that when means are removed the risk of suicide reduces.

Hopefully you will be supported through your teenager's safety plan. Ideally the safety plan will identify the likely triggers to look out for as well as what your teenager will do to keep safe. Your role in this should be clearly outlined so you have a mutually agreed plan. This will make it easier for you to feel confident in what to do. It will mean that your teenager will expect you to act as agreed, even if in the moment he or she is not wanting you to. If there's no plan in place, perhaps because your teenager hasn't engaged with a health professional, you could encourage him or her to use the BeyondNow suicide safety planning app from Beyondblue (www.beyondblue.org.au). You'll see that the safety plan includes the following sections with headings and ideas for completion:

- Warning signs

- Reasons to live

- Making the environment safe

- Things to do

- Connecting with people and places

- Friends and family to talk to

- Professional support.

The safety plan can be regularly reviewed and updated as things change. The idea of the safety plan is to help the young person plan ahead and take the actions identified in the plan. Seeing yourself as a support person who can facilitate ways for the teenager to stay safe will be helpful, although if the situation is escalating you may need to be more directive and act to keep them safe. If you have the support of a mental health professional you can ask specific questions about how to do this in helpful ways. Being confident in knowing what to do will also instil confidence in your teenager at the point of crisis.

Being prepared for those times when suicidal thoughts arise and having a series of realistic options to deal with them can prevent the young person moving towards suicidal acts as the only option to deal with how they're feeling. These options should include simple activities or actions that might help to self-soothe, distract the young person, or reach out to others. Having a number of options means that the young person is less likely to be reactive but rather able to focus on the activities knowing that there are other options if one doesn't work. Parents may become a key part of the safety plan and support the young person to work through the actions, but ultimately the young person needs to feel a sense of control and responsibility for the plan. The plan also includes reasons for living because ultimately we want to both prevent suicide from occurring and increase the young person's commitment to life. In essence the safety plan aims to be the lifeline that helps people to recognise the circumstances when they are likely to feel suicidal, ways they can deal with those feelings in the moment and who can help them. Importantly, the plan recognises that young people can experience suicidality quickly and can act impulsively.

If a situation arises where the mental health professional doesn't believe that there is sufficient substance in the safety plan under development or there is a lack of taking of responsibility for safety by the young person, he or she may need to review the level of need for the young person. While hospitalisation will be avoided as far as possible, if the mental health professional does not believe that the safety plan will be sufficient, there may be a need for hospitalisation to keep the young person safe for a short period of time. As mentioned earlier, hospitalisation is now kept as a last resort option because it removes the control and responsibility for the young person's safety away from them. Each state and territory will have legislations and procedures in relation to involuntary hospitalisation when a person is deemed unsafe. This is obviously a difficult scenario and ideally avoided as far as possible by intervening as early as concerns are raised to avoid the situation escalating.

Research has found that the period (for at least three months) after discharge from hospitalisation can be a period of risk for suicide. Careful planning following discharge from hospitalisation is therefore necessary, ideally with proactive outreach from mental health professionals for a period afterwards. Often this responsibility also falls to parents but increasingly there are services provided for follow up. It will be important to ask about these and link into what is available.

Chapter 11

Seeking ongoing help

One of the challenges for parents who are worried about their teenager's suicidality is getting the balance for safety and encouraging the teenager to take responsibility for themselves right. We may feel a pressing need to be monitoring behaviours and checking in regularly (or constantly). While there may be a time when this is appropriate (e.g., when the young person is actively suicidal or has just made a suicide attempt), once the immediate crisis settles this can be difficult (or impossible) for parents to sustain and can also be irritating for the young person. It can lead to conflict and a potential break down in the relationship if the young person feels like the parents are being overprotective. There is also the risk that the young person will become resentful and not share their suicidal thoughts with parents, thus creating what may be a more unsafe situation. Finding ways to build in check-ins but also helping the young person feel capable is essential. Hopefully the development of the safety plan is able to help the young person identify what kinds of support will be most helpful. Bear in mind also that it's not only parents who can be support people. The safety plan should include a range of people the young person feels comfortable talking with as well as helplines for phoning if necessary. Having many effective and trusted sources of support is better than relying on one source alone. Parents can sometimes feel like they are the only ones who can help or are responsible for keeping the young person safe. Talking about this in a way that expresses love and care rather than control will be most helpful. Sometimes sharing the responsibility can feel risky for parents so having a safety plan that clearly sets out responsibilities of parents and others can help to share the load and stop parents falling into the overresponsibility trap.

Communication and trust

As we've seen already, although it can seem to at the time, a suicidal crisis doesn't just arise from nowhere. It's common for people with suicidal thoughts (and not just teenagers) to keep these thoughts secret. Often there has been a period of struggle that may or may not have been visible to us and during that time communication and trust might have been breaking down. You'll remember from previous chapters that adolescence is a time when young people seek to become independent from their parents. As part of this change, communication will change and it can be incredibly difficult for parents to know what is happening for their teenagers, and particularly what is normal and what is becoming a concern. When our children are younger, they often seek us out when they are feeling sad or upset. We can be in tune with them to the point that we also can pick up on signs about how they are feeling even if they don't tell us. As they grow up, our job as parents has been to help them develop the skills to take more care of themselves. We expect them to tell us how they feel if they need to, but we also expect them to take more care of themselves, working out their own solutions and being able to deal with their feelings in better ways than when they were younger. What can be missed in this scenario, and we've covered this previously too, is the contradiction that as they grow and develop and look more capable, their brains are undergoing such significant changes that restrict their abilities to do all of the things we expect them to do. Add in a busy family life and pressures from school and friends and we have a perfect storm for struggles and breakdowns in communication. This is very common and has been the case for decades. It is now no doubt exacerbated by technological changes where young people are spending time using technology which removes them from the day to day conversations with parents. Now, it's important to recognise the various circumstances that have led to this point without blaming ourselves and becoming over-whelmed with guilt. Easier said than done I know.

We've explored the challenges parents face in their experience of par-enting a teenager who is suicidal. While they can have a range of feelings it's important that they find ways to keep communication open. Setting the scene to have conversations and finding ways to do this that fit in with your family's lifestyle will be necessary so they can work for your family's situa-tion. Finding genuine ways to connect will be important so the efforts don't seem token. This will take time and may not work as quickly or easily as you think, particularly when your teenager is feeling down and stressed. Breaking patterns of communication that have developed over a long period takes effort and time. Some questions to consider when planning how to do this:

- Look for connecting points — what do you both like to do? Or talk about? What interests do you share (or have shared in the past)?

- What are the simplest, cheapest ways you can connect with each other?

- How can you create space and time for each person in the family to have one-on-one time with parents as well as time as a family?

- When in the day are the best times to connect? Is it over breakfast or last thing at night?

- What have you noticed about your teenager's efforts to connect with you? When does this happen? What do they do? If they haven't done it recently, what have they done in the past?

- Given that technology is such an important part of life, how can it be used to help you connect?

- How can food make connection easier?

- Does going for a drive or a walk help the conversation flow more easily than sitting facing each other?

- Are there television shows or movies that you can watch together that you can both enjoy and talk about later?

- What might you need to give up for the moment in order to build these times and spaces for connection? What has got in the way of your connection?

- If your teenager was asked how they would like to connect with you, what would he or she say? Can you ask them? If not, why not? What concerns do you have?

When we are able to communicate more effectively we will be in a position to rebuild trust. Trust can break down when we feel like we have let each other down. We may feel like our teenager has let us down through their actions, and not telling us how they've been feeling. Our teenager, equally, may have felt let down if they attempted to tell us or seek help from us and felt unheard. Again this is good to know but to try not to feel guilty about. Guilt will close down the relationship and not enable trust to develop or be regained. It can help to think about how trust develops in a family situation. It's one of the essential elements of a family that's working well but it's very common for it to be tested during adolescence. The very nature of adolescent development where young people test boundaries and try out new ways of being tend to push the limits of trust. Parents can struggle with trusting their kids when they break curfews for example. From a teenager's point of view it can be difficult to feel that parents don't trust them and sometimes this can lead to resistance and rebellion. It can be easy for a vicious cycle of trust developing and breaking to occur. Finding ways to regain trust and work towards trusting again therefore are often important aspects of parenting with teenagers.

There are a few conditions which are essential for trust to be developed and maintained:

- *Unconditional love.* This seems like a natural way for parents to love their teenagers but can be difficult in reality. It can be easy for teenagers to feel like our love is conditional on them behaving well or doing things that the family can be proud of. Exploring what this means together can be critical to moving forward during difficult times, particularly if there have been arguments and critical or hurtful things said in the heat of the moment. It's another one of those paradoxes of parenting that often it's because of our love for our kids that we can come across as not caring about them or judging them.

- *Honesty.* This is the basis of positive relationships, of course, but often difficult during adolescence as teenagers start to keep some aspects of their lives private.

- *Reliability.* This can be as simple as following through on what we say we will do. Again this can sound simple but can break down quickly if circumstances change. Creating ways to communicate effectively if things change can help here. For example a short text message can be helpful.

- *Concern for the needs of others or empathy.* This requires the ability to think about what is going on for the other person and what they might need from you.

Plan for a return to school with support

School can be both a place of support and stress for young people. School is a place for a young person to socialise with peers and also connect with teachers and other school staff. Of course, it's a place for them to engage in life and learn, with a focus often towards the future, particularly in the latter years of secondary school. It can equally be a place of stress if school work is challenging or they have fallen behind. If they are struggling with friends or have been bullied it can be a place of isolation and struggle. We often hear about the culture of the school playing a role in how students feel welcomed and safe and this is critical. There is now considerable research that highlights the importance of school culture in the mental health and wellbeing of students. What your school calls it doesn't really matter but as a parent you'll recognise it as the feeling you get when you walk in the front door, the way you are noticed and made to feel important and the way any concerns you have are heard and responded to. Students similarly experience this in the way that teachers notice and speak with them, how ready they are to listen to concerns and take them seriously as well as how they notice interactions between students, acting promptly and effectively to any sign of bullying or harassment.

Ideally, you are in a situation where your teenager is keen to get back to school quickly and the school is eager to welcome him or her back and plan together how to provide support. The level of support required will vary depending on the time the teenager has been away, the level of distress currently felt, and how many people know about the current situation. If there hasn't been much school missed, things are settled and not many people know about the situation your teenager is likely to be able to return to school relatively easily. If your teenager is reluctant to return to school, however, it is essential to listen to concerns. Finding out what the school knows about any problems at school will be important too. You can ask your teenager which teacher or staff member knows them best and ask if they'd like you to contact them or whether they would like to be part of a meeting or telephone call with you. This is a time to be assertive about the need to take action but to balance this with ensuring that you are including your teenager in the discussion and plans as much as possible. It's one thing to get your teenager back to school, but it's entirely another thing for them to be wanting to be there and engaging in a way that is useful. I've worked with many kids as a school psychologist who turned up at school, entering through the front gate when dropped off by their parents to leave through the back gate a short time later. Schools are better these days at monitoring attendance so it's likely that this will be picked up quickly and the school will alert you, but generally speaking it's incredibly difficult to get your teenager to attend school if they don't want to be there or feel unsafe. Remembering this will help you to keep the focus on working with your teenager to come up with a plan. Listening to concerns first needs to be the starting point or the plan will just be words on a page that don't mean anything.

If your teenager is still experiencing some distress, the school may be reluctant to have him or her return. This is a very difficult situation because the school will be talking about their duty of care to your teenager and others in the school community, including all students and staff. They may be concerned that your teenager may harm themselves at school, they won't be able to keep him or her safe and that other students and staff may be affected. Thinking about this, you may also be reluctant to send your teenager somewhere that their safety cannot be guaranteed. At times like this it can be helpful to garner the support of a mental health professional. If your teenager is linked to a professional you could discuss this with them and ask them for advice and support in talking with the school. If not, you can ask the school for support from a student wellbeing staff member or mental health professional from the school to be part of discussions. Some of the important points to consider are listed below — focusing on what you, your teenager and the school have in common is a good starting point:

- School is an important part of a teenager's life and can be protective. It promotes a sense of routine and normality which is important during difficult times. School is a place that meets many of teenagers' learning, developmental, social and emotional needs.

- It is essential that the teenager feels and is safe. This includes safety in relation to suicide risk but also being safe from bullying or harassment. Having a clear safety plan can help in relation to the suicide risk. It may need to be adapted again to incorporate school-specific information (such as where to go if distressed, who can help, actions of school staff, etc.). Dealing with safety in relation to bullying or harassment will need a bigger discussion to ensure that the school is aware of what has been happening and is able to help your teenager (and you) feel confident that things will be different.

- When school staff, parents and the young person work together with mental health professionals to develop a plan to help the student return to school and keep safe, it is most likely to be successful.

- The longer the teenager is absent from school, the more difficult it will be for him or her to return, as he or she will miss school work as well as losing contact with peers.

- Changing schools can seem tempting and at times may be the answer, but it's important to try to work out any problems at the current school first. Listening to your teenager, however, and working with him or her to consider all options will also be important. Starting at a new school can have its challenges and some of the issues may also arise at the new school so careful planning will be important. Ultimately though we need to help the teenager feel heard and hopeful about the future.

Getting some broad agreement on the above can mean that you can then start to problem-solve a return to school. Being open to a gradual approach with regular reviews and monitoring might be the most useful way to plan the return. Talking with your teenager beforehand about their wishes as well as providing opportunities during any meetings for the teenager to voice their concerns or thoughts will be critical. Don't underestimate how difficult it can be for a young person to speak in a meeting of adults.

Planning beforehand how the teenager will be able to speak will help and this might include regular times where the teenager is asked what they think. If the young person does share their thoughts it's important that these are heard and validated. They need to be taken into account in the discussion and not just dismissed or ignored while the adults make all the decisions. It perhaps goes without saying but it helps to remember that it's the teenager who has to turn up to school and knows the situation best from their perspective. It can be easy for adults to make broad generalisations or assumptions that the teenager will experience as dismissive or disrespectful. Having a return to school plan that is documented will be helpful as agreements can sometimes be misconstrued or lost in the busy school environment. Having some time to review the plan and discuss it outside of the meeting will help before final agreement is made. The plan could include:

- A gradual return to school if necessary; perhaps half-days or attendance for certain periods to build confidence and get back into the routine of attending school full time. This might be necessary if there has been a lengthy period of time away from school or the teenager is reluctant to attend.

- Have more than one person to check in with on a daily basis initially then less often over time. It's essential to have more than one person as relying on one staff member can be problematic if they are away or get caught up and aren't available. The staff members chosen need to be people that the teenager feels comfortable with and can feel confident that they will be heard if there are concerns. The teenager can be included in planning about how this check in can happen, making sure it's private and the staff member is easy to find.

- Request that confidentiality is maintained as far as possible with staff only having the information they require. Also request that the school is alert to any gossip or rumours and acts quickly to stop these.

- Identify any specific concerns your teenager has, such as bullying or harassment and develop plans for responding to this. This may require school staff providing additional monitoring or talking to students about their behaviour. Making sure the teenager is included in these plans is essential so that he or she can trust that the school will handle it well. Empowering the teenager to deal with it as much as possible is important. It is reasonable for parents to ask school staff about ways that their anti-bullying or wellbeing policies are implemented as well as programs that aim to build positive relationships and processes to deal quickly with incidents of disrespect or bullying.

- Build in a way for the school to communicate with yourself and any mental health professionals involved. This may require more contact initially and then regular catch-ups over time. It can be useful to build in regular times even when things are going well to check in briefly so that issues don't get lost or escalate again. Don't underestimate how helpful it is to hear positive stories when things are going well. School staff and health professionals can be encouraged by these stories just as much as parents and their teenager. Building on small successes to keep the momentum going and plan to keep improving the situation can be so much more positive than finding yourself in a position where you must react to issues that have gone unchecked and spiralled quickly.

Role of families and friends

Regardless of professional help, parents, other family members and friends play a crucial role in supporting their teenager. While parents might feel helpless and believe that they aren't able to provide the help the young person needs, in fact the opposite may be true. The young person will benefit from having family members who are supportive and physically and emotionally present with them. You are the constant in their lives and know them better than anyone else. Even when the young person is seeing mental health professionals, family members will be the people the young person has day to day contact with. You are the people who will provide most of the support. This can at times feel overwhelming, particularly when you feel uncertain about what to do. Hopefully the mental health professionals have developed a safety plan and talked it through with you. Some of the questions that should be answered in the safety plan (and if not you can ask):

- If we are worried who can we call?

- What do we do if they say they want to hurt themselves?

- What if we find them hurting themselves?

- Can we leave them alone?

- When will the safety plan be reviewed?

These questions can help to tailor the safety plan for your particular family circumstances. Having these discussions with the mental health professionals and your teenager can help to develop some agreements and expectations about what will happen if the situation changes. This can help both you and your teenager to feel more confident that you will be able to cope. Sharing our concerns and having a plan can help us to think ahead and be prepared. Thinking about the feelings we might have can also help. This is called Psychological Preparedness and is an important way of acknowledging that we will face times of challenge and thinking ahead to help ourselves be prepared for those times. When we are prepared for a situation, we are better equipped to act quickly and negative impacts on us in the longer term in terms of our mental health can be reduced. Other questions you might want to discuss with the mental health professionals:

- Should we try to encourage our teenager to talk about feelings?

- What if they get angry with us?

- Should we encourage them to have their friends over?

- How will we know if they're spending too much time alone?

- Should we monitor social media use?

It is important to recognise that the better your relationship with your teenager, the more opportunity you will have to be part of the discussion. If your teenager doesn't want you to be part of the assessment and treatment planning the mental health professionals will not include you. This is particularly the case for young people who are 14 or 15 or older. This a tight rope for you to walk. On one hand your teenager has a right to confidentiality and treatment, yet you will be a critical support person for them. If you are responsible for their safety at home it is essential that you know what the safety plan is. Remember to give your teenager as much control as possible over the plan and what your role is. They will be feeling out of control and scared and may push you away as part of this. By listening and asking rather than telling you may be more likely to be included in discussions and planning. This is another reason however that you need to be assertive in seeking your own support. Part of your challenge will be to find a way to manage your worry and anxiety about your teenager's safety while also helping them to feel confident in their own abilities to manage their own feelings and make safe decisions. It is their ability to keep themselves safe that ultimately will keep them safe so anything that disempowers them will not be helping to achieve this aim.

Help your teenager continue to build their problem solving capacity

This is something that you will have been working on with your teenager since they were a young child, so it won't be new. What might be new or different is that they need to do this more for themselves now, within the midst of confusion and emotions that come with adolescence. You might be tempted to think that they should know how to do this, that some ways of resolving problems are obvious. Remember that their brain development means that this may not be as easy as it looks and when distressed with suicidal thoughts it's common for funnel thinking to kick in which reduces the capacity to think of all options. Making decisions when emotions are heightened is difficult for us all.

Helping them to think through the steps of making decisions and working through problems can be something that you model and work with them on a day-to-day basis. Being patient with them and showing that there is always a range of options for any problem can be helpful. One of those options is that they can always ask others for help if they need more ideas.

Chapter 12

Mental health diagnoses and types of interventions

Working with mental health professionals

Y ou may or may not have seen a mental health professional, such as a psychologist, before. While we've been working to improve the stigma about mental health for decades and encouraging people to feel comfortable to seek help from psychologists and other mental health professionals, the reality is that it can still be difficult for people to do this. Perhaps we tend to think we can handle things or at least want to try to handle things and it's only when we reach a point where we realise that we can't that we then seek help. At that point we can feel like we've failed and seeing a mental health professional can represent that failure. This happens in the context of stigma that can still be present despite years of awareness raising activities. If we use a physical health comparison, we know that the earlier we get concerns checked out the more likely we are to catch things before they get worse, have more options for treatment and often to feel better because we have done something about the problem. The same can apply for mental health concerns.

We absolutely know that seeking help as early as possible is very important. For children and young people this can mean early in age as well as early in terms of signs of concern. It's particularly important because mental health concerns can impact on the development of children and young people. It's easy, however, to get caught up in the confusion about what might be a 'stage' or 'phase' of development and what might actually be a sign of an emerging mental health issue. This is challenging to tease out because many of the behaviours are the same and when you combine that with the teenager's personality and life circumstances there's a bit to untangle. As a parent we are part of that tangle, bringing our personality, reflections, and life experiences too. That's why it's so useful to look to a mental health professional to help. By seeing the situation from a neutral and distant place and bringing to bear their training and previous experiences of working with other families, they can bring a whole new perspective to increase our understandings. They can ask questions to get us thinking about those things we tend to ignore or not be aware of. These questions and observations can help to lift the lid on what is happening for us. As long as we are open to the experience, this can lead to new insights that can help us to understand what is going on more easily. Sometimes this is difficult because we tend to shut out what is difficult for us to face.

Each mental health professional will have their own approach to the way they work with you and your teenager. I can speak best about the way that psychologists typically work so I'll outline this to give you an idea of what to expect. For teenagers over the age of 14 or 15 years the young person will likely to be able to give informed consent to the assessment and treatment. The psychologist is likely to spend a fair bit of time gathering information from you and your teenager. They might want to see you as a family as well as individually. It is important that the psychologist sees the young person without parents and that confidentiality is assured so that the young person feels comfortable sharing information. They might also ask permission to speak to the teenager's school. This may take some time and it can be frustrating when we want answers to our concerns and yet the psychologist just seems to be asking more and more questions. It can take a few sessions also for people to feel comfortable talking openly with the psychologist, what we might call the building of rapport. This relates to trust and also the unfamiliarity we can have when reflecting on our lives, our thoughts and our feelings. Of course, if there are immediate safety concerns, the psychologist will focus on that and work to develop the safety plan that we've talked about previously. For longer term support, however, more information is needed. The psychologist may be working towards what is called a 'case formulation'. This is an approach which brings together the training and skills of the psychologist with the information you provide across the following areas:

1. Presenting problem — current key concern or problem that brought you to see the psychologist (which may not end up being the actual concern or problem)

2. Predisposing factors — vulnerabilities or factors that predispose the person to develop the problem

3. Precipitating factors — stressors or triggers that have impacted to lead to the problem at this time

4. Perpetuating factors — maintaining factors that keep the problem occurring

5. Positive factors — strengths and capacities that can be built upon to help resolve the situation.

Through gathering this information in a systematic way the psychologist can develop with you and your teenager a hypothesis about what is happening at the moment, what has led to this situation arising and what will therefore be the best way forward to resolve the situation. Hopefully through this process you and your teenager can gain a better understanding of what is going on and what might have contributed to it. It's likely that there's more than one perspective with you all bringing different aspects to the way you see the situation. It helps to understand the family as a dynamic, where the experiences or behaviour of one family member impacts on the others.

Importantly, the idea is not to lay blame or use the information to criticise anyone but to really understand what is happening so that the way forward will be clearer and any efforts to improve the situation will be realistic and can be sustained over time. Rushing too quickly into solutions can mean that important underlying factors are overlooked and simplistic responses can be developed which lead to a rebounding of problems later. For some people that can mean jumping from crisis to crisis. It is important to trust the process and recognise that the situation took time to develop, so will take time to resolve. Focusing on small steps or goals and recognising efforts and achievements will help you feel like progress is being made.

The psychologist might also ask you to complete a family genogram. This can be a time effective way for the psychologist to get a sense of the family, family history, relationships between members as well as historical factors which might form part of the predisposing factors mentioned above. Sometimes we aren't aware that there are family values, beliefs and experiences that flow through generations, which can lead to patterns of behaviour that we take for granted. We will all have blind spots and see some of the ways we do things as normal because it's the way our family has always been. Having a psychologist explore this with us can help these become illuminated. Once we recognise these we can start to understand some of the unspoken rules and ways of doing things that might be contributing to challenges for us.

Once the assessment has been completed the psychologist may provide you with an overview of how things seem to him or her. This is a chance for you and your teenager to let the psychologist know what makes sense to you or whether there are other things you think need to be factored in, or whether some things have been given too much weight. Ideally this is a collaborative process where you work together to make sense of what is going on. Sometimes this can be challenging. We all have things in our lives that we prefer not to think much about or to diminish the importance of. Being open and ready to hear and trust what the psychologist, as a skilled practitioner who is external to the situation, has to say will help you to face the reality of what is happening. It's only from that position that you can move forward and develop plans that will actually work.

Depending on the way the psychologist works this discussion might include a diagnosis or provisional diagnosis, such as depression or anxiety. If so, they might then propose a treatment plan based on the current evidence about what has been shown through research to treat the disorder. Some psychologists might be less open to a diagnosis, particularly for younger adolescents, but may come up with a treatment plan related to the symptoms and concerns raised during the assessment period. The Safety Plan will continue to be reviewed while the treatment plan is implemented so that the focus on safety is not lost.

Having a plan for you to keep in contact with the mental health professional, particularly during stressful periods, will be critical. You might find that this needs to be more often initially but over time, as other supports come into place, the sessions can reduce. The psychologist should be able to work with you and your teenager as part of the safety plan to identify how and when to make contact with them. Having other contact details will be important too, particularly for emergencies. Finding ways to keep in touch with the psychologist to provide updates and seek support for meetings with the school will also be important. The more responsibility your teenager can take for this contact the better, but you will also need to be in the loop of this and feel confident that the communication channels are open. You may also want to talk to the psychologist about seeking support for yourself. While the psychologist will likely be keen to see you as part of the family of your teenager, remember that their primary focus will be on your teenager. They will be able to recommend colleagues who can see you for your own support. It's important that these are kept separate, so that you can all have the opportunity to talk openly and freely about how things are going for you.

You will be guided by the mental health professional in relation to what treatment or intervention will be most helpful for your teenager. This intervention will initially focus on assessment and safety planning, particularly when the teenager reports having suicidal thoughts. The assessment process may have provided some useful information about your teenager's needs that can be prioritised and built into a treatment plan.

Getting a mental health diagnosis

Research suggests that the majority of people who die by suicide have signs of a diagnosable mental health condition, although they may not necessarily have been diagnosed formally. While the focus will necessarily be on keeping your teenager safe and dealing with the immediate crisis, it is likely that your teenager will also be referred to a mental health professional for a comprehensive mental health assessment to explore this possibility. For some young people there can be an immediate stressor that has led to the suicidal thoughts or behaviour and once this is known and efforts made to deal with it the risk can subside. The focus for assessment might also be on ways of coping with strong feelings and whether there is an underlying mental health issue that is impacting on that. A comprehensive assessment should look at the young person's development, personality, life history, coping in a range of situations and beliefs about their life. Parents can provide useful information, particularly about development and childhood experiences, so ideally will be able to be included in the assessment process. The focus will also be on the current experiences of the young person so it will be necessary for the mental health professional to see the young person on their own as well. Even when we have positive relationships with our kids, there will be some aspects of their lives that are private and they won't want to share in front of us. In order to be able to work effectively with the young person, it is necessary that the mental health professional knows what is going on for the young person, their concerns and issues facing them. Focus on the importance of the young person in getting help rather than on you being included in all discussions. Trust also that the mental health professional will work with the young person to encourage him or her to share anything important with you (and of course any concerns in relation to current safety of the young person or others will be shared with you).

It can be helpful to know that there are currently debates about whether suicide risk should always be seen as part of a mental health condition and the focus should be on treatment for that or whether the suicidality itself needs treatment. Increasingly, treatments for the suicide risk itself are seen to be a priority, but a comprehensive mental health assessment will help to understand any underlying factors that might be impacting and ensure that the best evidence-based treatment is made available for both short and long-term treatment. By treating any mental health disorders, the young person will be better equipped to manage and the risk of suicide is likely to reduce over time. A focus just on the mental health disorder though without exploring what is leading to current suicidal thoughts or behaviour can risk losing sight of the most immediate concerns and leave the young person at risk. This all needs careful management by a mental health professional who is experienced in working with young people, is confident dealing with suicidality and is well supported by their own support network (e.g., supervisors).

It is well recognised that the most important part of any mental health treatment is the development of a trusting relationship (sometimes referred to as the 'therapeutic alliance') between the young person and the mental health professional. If the young person doesn't feel supported or can't develop trust in the professional, they are not likely to want to attend appointments or to get the most out of the sessions. You may be able to help your teenager explore this, without judgement as much as possible. Exploring options together if it doesn't seem to be working can be a key role for you to play. Encouraging the young person to talk honestly with the professional about their needs and what is helping or not is another way you can help. This can be difficult to do. Practising ways of saying it or offering to attend a session to support the young person could work. While it can feel like you are criticising the mental health professional by sharing these concerns, you may find that the mental health professional is pleased to have the conversation and will be keen to find a way to enhance the relationship and improve the situation so that the sessions are more effective. If, after raising these concerns and exploring possible solutions, your teenager is still reluctant to attend or isn't finding it helpful, it will be important to look for another mental health professional.

When looking for a mental health professional, consider the following with your teenager to try to tease out who will be most helpful. This can be easier to work out after having seen a mental health professional previously:

- Gender.
- Age.
- Cultural background.
- The way the professional works (e.g., activities, talking, homework).
- Treatment modality — the young person may not be aware of this so it's worth asking for an explanation about the underlying approach to treatment.
- Whether there is an expectation that the parents will see the mental health professional for some sessions or parts of sessions.
- Where the young person can see the mental health professional (e.g., close to home, setting and how youth friendly it is (e.g., GP's clinic, school, private practice).

You may like to talk with your teenager about what they think will be most helpful for them before you make contact with a mental health professional.

This might give you an idea about what the young person expects will happen, including any concerns they have or misconceptions. Once you've listened to these, you might be able to clarify some of them or encourage the young person to clarify these directly with the mental health professional. If, for example, your teenager expects that they'll see someone who will just tell them what they should do, you can clarify that this isn't what the mental health professional will do. They will work together with the young person to work out what will be most helpful. The mental health professional may ask a lot of questions to get a good understanding of what is happening at the start but ideally the young person is doing a lot of the talking and will feel heard and come away with new ideas.

There are a number of mental health disorders which may be present when young people have suicidal thoughts or have attempted suicide. It can be useful to understand that suicidality can occur within the context of the distress associated with the mental illness. Sometimes it can help young people to have a name that describes how they are feeling or what they are experiencing. Some of the most common mental health disorders experienced by adolescents and young adults with their typical symptoms are listed below: I've included this basis description of the disorders to give you an idea of the types of patterns of symptoms that make up these disorders. It's important that you don't use this to make any decisions about a disorder that your teenager has, as there needs to be a comprehensive assessment before a diagnosis is made. Having some of these symptoms doesn't mean that the disorder will be diagnosed as there is a strict set of criteria a person needs to meet before the diagnosis is made by a mental health professional (although some GPs will also make diagnoses of mental health disorders).

Depression
Depression can cause changes in thinking, how a young person responds to things, motivation and activity levels, sleep, and relationships. There are different types of depression (e.g., major depressive disorder, persistent depressive disorder or dysthymia or depression related to alcohol and other drugs), but typical symptoms include:

- Feelings of irritability or unhappiness for most of the day — could be described as 'numbness' or 'emptiness'

- Less interested and pleasure in activities that were once enjoyed

- Significant changes in appetite and weight

- Sleep changes — not being able to sleep (insomnia) or sleeping more than usual (hypersomnia)

- Restlessness and agitation

- Being tired and feeling fatigued without energy nearly every day

- Feeling bad, worthless, hopeless or guilty with feelings of self-blame or self-criticism

- Problems with concentration, memory, and making decisions

- Preoccupation with dark and gloomy themes and thoughts of death or suicide.

Anxiety

Anxiety is a feeling of worry or nervousness that becomes a problem when it is intense, causes distress, lasts for a prolonged period of time and affects daily living. There are a number of anxiety disorders, including social anxiety disorder, panic disorder, agoraphobia, generalised anxiety disorder and separation anxiety disorder. Although symptoms will vary depending upon the type of disorder, symptoms include:

- Persistent worry

- Seeking excessive reassurance, avoiding making decisions

- Excessive fearfulness

- Inability to relax

- Problems with sleep

- Avoidance of feared situations

- Excessive shyness

- Social isolation and problems with relationships, avoiding situations and not spending time with friends or family

- Difficulty concentrating and making decisions

- Fear of social embarrassment

- Problems with work, social and family life

- Physical symptoms, such as stomach aches, headaches, muscle soreness, sweating, nausea and diarrhoea

- Nightmares

- Panic attacks

- Expressing anxious thoughts about themselves, their situation or future (e.g., 'I can't cope', 'I'll make a fool of myself', 'They won't like me', 'What if something bad happens', 'I might get hurt').

Bipolar disorder

Bipolar disorder is a chronic mental health condition with strong changes in mood and energy. People experiencing bipolar disorder can experience:

- Depressive episodes: low mood, feelings of hopelessness, extreme sadness and lack of interest and pleasure in things.

- Manic or hypomanic episodes: extremely high mood and activity or agitation, racing thoughts little need for sleep and rapid speech.

These changes in mood can last a week or more, and affect thoughts and behaviour, affecting how the person is able to function in everyday life. People experience bipolar disorder in different ways. Untreated, it makes it hard to consistently cope at home, school/work or socially. Someone with bipolar disorder has episodes of depression and highs (feeling 'hyper' or wired).

During the depressed phase symptoms may include:

- Feelings of sadness or hopelessness

- Loss of interest in usually pleasurable activities

- Withdrawal from family and friends

- Sleep problems (often excessive sleep)

- Loss of energy, feeling exhausted

- Physical slowing

- Low self-esteem

- Feelings of guilt

- Problems concentrating

- Suicidal thoughts.

During the 'highs' they might feel like things are speeding up, they can have thousands of thoughts and ideas and may feel invincible or behave recklessly. Symptoms during this manic phase may include:

- Feeling incredibly 'high' or euphoric

- Delusions of self-importance

- High levels of creativity, energy and activity

- Getting much less sleep or no sleep

- Poor appetite and weight loss

- Racing thoughts, racing speech, talking over people

- Highly irritable, impatient or aggressive

- Inappropriate sexual activity or risk taking

- Dressing more colourfully and being less inhibited

- Impulsive and making poor choices in spending or business

- Grand and unrealistic plans

- Poor concentration, easily distracted

- Delusions, hallucinations.

Bipolar disorder can be difficult to diagnose because its onset is often noticed during the depressive phase and people often report the depressive symptoms more than the mania or hypomania symptoms. Therefore, it's easy to misdiagnose bipolar disorder as depression.

Borderline personality disorder

People affected by borderline personality disorder (BPD) have difficulty managing their emotions and impulses, relating to people and maintaining a stable self-image. It can be highly distressing for the person affected, and often for their family and friends too. It can be confusing and easily misunderstood, but is a very treatable condition.

People with BPD typically experience some, but not necessarily all, of these symptoms:

- Feeling empty, low self-esteem

- Paranoia or emotional detachment

- Anxiety about relationships, efforts to avoid being abandoned

- Impulsive, risky behaviour

- Self-harm, threatening or attempting suicide

- Anger, moodiness, irritability.

Eating disorders

An eating disorder is a serious mental illness, characterised by eating, exercise and body weight or shape becoming an unhealthy preoccupation of a person's life. Eating disorders can take many different forms and interfere with a person's day-to-day life. Four eating disorders are currently recognised: anorexia nervosa, bulimia nervosa, binge eating disorders and other eating disorders. It can be difficult to notice the signs or symptoms of an eating disorder, but some of the behavioural, physical and psychological signs are provided in the following lists.

Behavioural warning signs:

- Constant or repetitive dieting

- Evidence of binge eating

- Evidence of vomiting or laxative abuse

- Excessive or compulsive exercise patterns

- Making a list of 'good' and 'bad' foods

- Changes in food preferences

- Development of patterns or obsessive rituals around food preparation and eating

- Avoidance of all social situations involving food

- Frequent avoidance of eating meals by giving excuses
- Behaviours focused around food preparation and planning
- Strong focus on body shape and weight
- Development of repetitive or obsessive body checking behaviours
- Social withdrawal or isolation from friends, including avoidance of previously enjoyed activities
- Change in clothing style, such as wearing baggy clothes
- Deceptive behaviour around food
- Eating very slowly
- Continual denial of hunger.

Physical warning signs:

- Sudden or rapid weight loss
- Frequent changes in weight
- Sensitivity to the cold
- Loss or disturbance of menstrual periods
- Signs of frequent vomiting
- Fainting, dizziness
- Fatigue.

Psychological warning signs:

- Increased preoccupation with body shape, weight and appearance
- Intense fear of gaining weight
- Constant preoccupation with food or with activities relating to food
- Extreme body dissatisfaction/negative body image
- Distorted body image
- Heightened sensitivity to comments or criticism about body shape or weight, eating or exercise habits

- Heightened anxiety around meal times

- Depression or anxiety

- Moodiness or irritability

- Low self-esteem

- Rigid 'black and white' thinking (viewing everything as either 'good' or 'bad')

- Feelings of life being 'out of control'

- Feelings of being unable to control behaviours around food.

Psychosis

Psychosis is a term for a range of symptoms where a person's beliefs, thoughts, feelings, senses and behaviours are altered. This can cause someone to misinterpret or confuse what's happening around them. An episode of psychosis is a period where someone has more intense or severe symptoms of psychosis that last for more than a week and that interfere with their day-to-day life. Most people have a period of time leading up to the onset of an episode of psychosis in which they start to experience these symptoms, but less frequently or less severely. Psychosis can occur as part of mental health disorders such as schizophrenia, bipolar disorder, major depressive disorder, schizophreniform disorder, as part of a medical condition or related to substance use. Symptoms vary from person to person and can change over time and include:

- Confused thinking.

- False beliefs or delusions.

- Hallucinations — when a person sees, hears, feels, smells or tastes something that's not actually there.

- Changed feelings, including mood swings, feeling strange or cut off from the world or as if everything is moving in slow motion.

- Changed behaviour where the person behaves differently to usual. They may be extremely active or tired, may laugh when things don't seem funny or become upset or angry for no clear reason.

Getting an accurate diagnosis

You will see from the above lists of symptoms and warning signs that there is a lot of overlap between them across the diagnoses. The lists are provided to give you a starting point for exploration whether or not your teenager might meet the criteria for the diagnosis. Careful assessment will be required to gather information to rule in or out a particular diagnosis. This takes time and a willingness for your teenager to engage with the mental health professional. You may also be asked to provide some information (e.g., developmental history and current symptoms that you can see), as there will be some aspects of their history and current behaviours that the young person may not be fully aware of. The more information the professional has the more likely it will be that an accurate diagnosis will be made. Sometimes the young person may have some of the symptoms but not meet all of the criteria required to gain the diagnosis. In young teenagers, sometimes, the professional will provide a provisional diagnosis rather than a more definite diagnosis. In any event, the diagnosis will help to make sense of the symptoms and also help to determine what interventions or treatments will be most effective. Sometimes teenagers and their parents find this useful and comforting but sometimes it can be difficult to hear that there is a mental health diagnosis that fits. Careful management of this will be required to support the young person in understanding what it means and how it can be helpful. Look out for signs that the young person is minimising their symptoms or acting out their symptoms in response to the diagnosis.

Treatments for suicidality

Research suggests that treatments that focus only on mental health issues may not be sufficiently specific to the mechanisms that give rise to suicidal behaviour. This means they may treat the symptoms of the mental health issue but not necessarily the risk for suicide attempts. The treatment plan is therefore likely to address underlying mental health issues, family issues or other relevant concerns that may have been identified, as well as suicide-specific concerns. For example, a person may have a diagnosis of depression and appropriately receive treatment for that, however, if the person in response to challenging situations attempts suicide, they will need more intensive treatment support that addresses their suicidality as well. This may include a focus on self-regulation and coping, for example. It is important then that the suicide-specific concerns are identified and addressed along with any underlying mental health issue. Having suicidal symptoms may only partly be explained by the mental health diagnosis.

Depending upon the approach of the mental health practitioner, the following types of treatments may be provided:

- Treatments where the family is the primary focus of the intervention (e.g., attachment-based family therapy)

- Treatments focused on individual skills training and augmented treatment with family therapy sessions

- Treatments where the teenager is the main focus of the intervention and family sessions are optional or not presented as integral to the treatment plan.

There are a number of interventions that are now gaining credibility with emerging evidence of success in working with adolescents who are suicidal. It is important to note that research is still exploring how these work and what other interventions may be beneficial. Here's a brief summary of those interventions with good evidence that they will work to reduce suicidal behaviours, particularly suicidal thoughts. This information can provide you with a starting point in discussing the treatment with your teenager's mental health professional and also help you understand something about the treatment to be ready to talk about it with your teenager if they wish to.

Cognitive–behaviour therapy (CBT) for suicide prevention

CBT has been shown to be effective in reducing recurrence of suicidal behaviours with larger effects in adults compared with adolescents, individual compared to group settings and when suicidality is an explicit treatment focus. Components of CBT designed to specifically address suicidality include:

- Chain analysis

- Psychoeducation

- Addressing reasons for living and building hope

- Case conceptualisation in order to inform skill building (within this, standard CBT techniques can be used such as behavioural activation, mood monitoring, emotion regulation and distress tolerance, cognitive restructuring, problem solving, goal setting, building social support and assertiveness skills)

- Family sessions

- Relapse prevention.

Dialectical behaviour therapy (DBT)

DBT is probably the most commonly investigated psychotherapy for recurrent suicidal behaviours. It promotes self-efficacy, interpersonal effectiveness and emotional regulation, and has repeatedly been shown to reduce the recurrence of suicidal behaviours compared to treatment as usual. DBT was developed by Marsha Linehan and originally developed to treat women with personality disorders who engaged in suicidal behaviour. Teaching skills that help people to regulate and tolerate their emotions can help people who are suicidal as they can have difficulty labelling, tolerating and regulating emotions.

Mentalisation-based therapy

This therapy is derived from psychodynamic theory in which the client is taught how to conceptualise actions in terms of thoughts and feelings. It has been shown to be effective in reducing suicidal behaviours, particularly in adults. Adolescents vulnerable to emotion dysregulation and self-harm often have deficits in the ability to mentalise: to understand, acknowledge, and predict thoughts and feelings in oneself and others. It includes psychoeducation and coping strategies that may be useful to reduce suicidal behaviours.

Attachment-based family therapy

This therapy emerges from interpersonal theories that suggest adolescent depression and suicide can be precipitated, exacerbated or buffered against by the quality of interpersonal relationships in families. It is a trust-based, emotion-focused psychotherapy model that aims to repair interpersonal ruptures and rebuild an emotionally protective, secure-based parent–child relationship.

Medications

There are debates about the appropriateness of medications related to mental health for adolescents, with some research suggesting that antidepressant treatment is associated with a risk of new-onset or worsening suicidal ideation or suicide attempts. Alerts about these concerns were first raised in the United States in 2004 when a Black Box Warning about the possibility of increased suicidality associated with antidepressants in young people (Friedman, 2014). This led to considerable caution in Australia in relation to the prescribing of antidepressants for young people under 25 years of age. Besides antidepressants, other pharmacological interventions used in mood disorders have shown some benefit on suicidal behaviour, although many studies showing these benefits were not conducted with young people. Discussions about the appropriateness of medications need to take place with a medical practitioner, such as a psychiatrist, paediatrician or general practitioner with specialist and current knowledge in relation to adolescent mental health. In any event, evidence is clear that medication is most beneficial with psychological therapy.

School-based interventions

In addition to counselling and support that may be in place for young people in the school setting, there are mental health awareness programs that have been found to be beneficial as part of a whole-school approach which includes training for staff, and good referral processes for mental health support. One such program that has been adapted for use in Australia is the Youth Aware of Mental Health (YAM), which is a mental health and suicide prevention program for 14 to 16 year olds that builds students' knowledge of mental health through role-play and interactive discussion. In European trials, YAM has been shown to reduce depression and anxiety, suicide attempts and severe suicidal ideation (Wasserman, et. al., 2015). YAM also helps young people connect with local mental and general health resources as well as organisations who work with young people.

Chapter 13

Self-care and seeking help for yourself

I f your teenager is reluctant to see someone you can always seek help for yourself so that you can be better informed and looking after yourself during this difficult period. While you are focused on getting help for your teenager, you will also be experiencing your own stress and probably feelings of being overwhelmed. For some parents, this can trigger memories of their own previous struggles and fears can escalate in response to that. If you have family members who have died of suicide it may be difficult to get that out of your mind and you may be stuck with the worry that this will happen to your teenager as well. All these thoughts and feelings can impact on how we respond to our teenager. It can feel impossible to separate this out. If you want to see a mental health professional, you will need to see someone who hasn't seen your teenager as there needs to be separation in roles. If your teenager is seeing someone you could ask them for suggestions for someone who could help you. This is often a good place to start and can help us feel confident that the person will be a good fit for us and can be easier than ringing someone cold.

You may decide to let your teenager know that you are going to see someone or you may choose to keep this private, particularly if you are not sure how your teenager will react. You will want to be careful not to make it sound like the teenager's experience is all about you. They will be focused on their own needs and feelings and will want those validated rather than hearing about how their behaviour is affecting you or causing them distress. Even though they may not say it, they may be well aware of the effect on you and feeling guilty about it. On the other hand, if we do let the young person know that we are seeking help, we are modelling good self-care and this might be helpful in normalising help-seeking. It's therefore important to think through what to share, how to frame it and the best time to share this information.

During sessions with a mental health professional you may explore how you are feeling and responding to the situation as well as get some help to come up with some ideas about what else you might be able to do to support your teenager. They obviously won't know what is going on exactly for your teenager so they will want to focus on how you are responding and feeling, rather than providing advice about what your teenager needs. For some parents this support can provide them with a way to manage their emotions and worries so that they are better equipped to continue to support their teenager. This might help with self-awareness about how our own experience and behaviour can play out and impact on the teenager. It might also mean that they feel calmer when having conversations with their teenager and more able to broach what are difficult discussions about the risk of suicide attempts.

Seeing a mental health professional might also help you understand the experience of getting professional support and how to encourage your teenager to do so. You might be able to gain a perspective of what it is like to go through this process, as well as what is difficult about seeking help. Taking the time to focus on yourself can also help you to consider all of the other aspects of your life that may be impacted by your teenager's current situation. It can help you to gain perspective on the effects on your other children, your partner, extended family, friends and work. You might find the opportunity to problem solve ways to manage each of these situations rather than use your usual ways that may or may not be helpful in the uniqueness of this situation. Accessing professional support can help us to challenge some of our long-held beliefs about ourselves and our role as parent. It can help us to give ourselves permission to focus on ourselves and prioritise what is most important at that point in time. This might mean reducing some of our usual commitments for a period of time. The health professional might also help us to tackle our greatest fears, particularly the worry about losing our teenager. These are not easy to face and that's why it's so important to find a mental health professional that you can connect well with and trust. Sometimes we don't recognise just how our feelings are showing to others or affecting what we say and do. You might also find that you can talk through any feelings of responsibility, guilt and shame that are arising for you. Putting names to these feelings can help to normalise them and defuse their power. Looking at your role as a parent, its limitations and the strengths and capacities you have can be affirming but also help you be realistic about what you can and cannot do.

One of the biggest challenges for parents can be maintaining their own interests and identity. Giving ourselves permission to do things just for ourselves when our children seem so needy can be challenging. We can receive a lot of messages about what a 'good parent' does or doesn't do. Often we see images or stories of good parents being there for their kids and this is true. What is often missing from these images or stories is how parents can only continue to be there for their kids if they have their own self-care mechanisms in place. Parents can't keep giving when they are, to use a car analogy, running on empty. They need to refuel on a regular basis and they need to use fuel of a sufficient quality to make sure the engine runs well. Snatching a few moments to do something for themselves here and there, rather than having this time built in to their life, is likely to lead to both physical and mental health risks. Sometimes when I worked with parents in groups this was one of the most important learnings for the participants. Sometimes they had neglected their own basic health needs. For example, some of them decided to have a physical health check-up after realising that they had spent so much time caring for their kids that they'd neglected their own basic health maintenance. At times, this did reveal underlying health issues that had been glossed over as tiredness. For others, it was recognising the need to invest in their relationships with adults, including partners. This often meant giving themselves permission to prioritise spending solid of blocks of time with adults without the kids.

Prioritising time for ourselves often means needing to communicate this to others, perhaps to seek their support to enable this to occur. Feeling confident enough to have this conversation can be a challenge, particularly if this is the first time this has been discussed. It can be helpful to identify times when you have felt worn out or that you haven't been as fully present as you could be. It will help to convince yourself first that spending time caring for yourself is important before you talk to anyone else about it, although finding a supportive person to discuss it with first could help you to identify the ways that a lack of self-care is impacting on you. Some of the signs you could look out for:

- Physical illness — particularly immune system problems, like getting lots of colds, feelings of exhaustion, stomach upsets, headaches, aches and pains as muscles tense up.

- Changes in appetite and sleep patterns — more or less than usual.

- Episodes of shallow breathing — feelings of panic.

- Tiredness — perhaps because your sleep is disrupted or your diet is missing some key nutrients.

- Mind wandering, racing thoughts or confusion — having so many thoughts that you can't concentrate on any one thing at a time, feeling overwhelmed or fixated on worries. This can lead to a lack of confidence and inability to make decisions.

- Misunderstandings or misinterpretations — may be caused by not fully tuning in or understanding what the other person is saying. Can lead to conflicts.

- Agitation, lack of patience or irritability — could be related to all the earlier signs.

You may know yourself well enough to know which of these signs, or other symptoms, are most likely to affect you. They are the same signs that a person experiencing burnout in a workplace could feel and if not dealt with well, over time can build up to lead to mental health problems as well as physical health issues. Of course it's natural that at times of pressure you will be wanting to prioritise your teenager and that's important but look also for opportunities to regularly do small things that help you feel like you are taking back some control of your life and prioritising your own needs when you can. They don't have to be big things, just small things that mark the moment and tell yourself and others that you are important. This is where allowing others to care for you can give you the space to do something for yourself. You'll notice that taking some time for yourself can help you to process your thoughts and feelings so that you can gain a different perspective.

Examples of small ways to care for yourself include:

- Enjoy a bubble bath before bed.

- Read a book for half an hour instead of household tasks.

- Write a journal; writing a small amount each day can become a habit where feelings and thoughts can be expressed. You can use a physical diary or set up a space on your mobile phone or tablet.

- Keep a 'Gratitude Diary' and every morning writing three things you are grateful for can help your day start off positively and give you a focus.

- Plan to take a course or start or revisit a hobby when you have more time. Break the planning down into steps and relish the opportunity to look forward to do something you will enjoy.

- Make time for a coffee catch up with a friend you haven't seen for a while (or make an appointment to Skype or Facetime if they're not physically close by).

- Identify one night each week when you prioritise your own time. It could be a television show you like or an interest that you want to pursue. You may need to plan this ahead and get some support to make this happen. Perhaps begin with one night a month and build on it when you can.

Like our teenagers, we are social beings. Being alone with a problem makes it harder to bear. When we are parenting we become so close to the situation that it's pretty much impossible to be objective. Seeking help can mean connecting with others who have been through or are going through a similar experience. When I ran parenting programs, they sometimes became support groups or facilitated self-help groups. Often when parents got together in a formal setting they were able to experience being with other parents in a safe space to share their experiences, admit their feelings without fear of judgement and to explore together the way forward. As a facilitator of these groups I often felt that the essence of the work was in the way these parents supported each other, not from any remarkable skills or insight I was passing on. It was their social need to connect, to be with others, to feel understood and heard that was valued. This often gave them the strength to return home with some degree of renewed hope. I came to believe that my job in these groups was to set up an environment that could be hope-giving, that could enable the parents to feel understood and to have the courage to face another day with their teenagers.

We can't support a teenager who is suicidal all on our own. We need some space to reflect on our own experience, time to do some things we enjoy and keep a sense of containment in our lives. Our teenager needs to feel a team of support around them too, rather than a heavy reliance on one person. This is a testing time, with our relationship with our teenager becoming intense. We can't let ourselves feel like we are the only ones holding this together. You might find it helpful to grab a piece of paper and reflect on the village around your family. Who are the people who support you? Begin to make a list and then take a look at it. What do you notice?

- Who are the people you can talk to easily about your worries?

- Who are the people who won't judge, won't give you simplistic solutions?

- Who are the people who will listen to you, be there for you regardless of what the problem is?

As you think critically about the people on your list you might begin to cross some people off. Some people aren't able to understand this particular situation or will want to help you so much that they will jump in and try to solve the problem for you. Some just won't be able to see your perspective. You might like to move those people to a different list. Those people can still be supportive and fun to be with but they're not the people you know you can rely on at the most critical times.

You might be able to think about people who have been through their own battles with their kids or their own mental health. They might work with young people or have a good understanding of the situations parents and teenagers find themselves in. These are the people who will be most able to listen to you but also make some suggestions when you are ready to hear them. Be careful too that they don't tell you what you should do. Remember that every situation can be different and you will work out what you need to do in your unique situation.

You might be looking at your list and thinking you don't have anyone you are confident can be there for you at this time. You may have friends with younger kids who just won't understand what's happening for you. And you mightn't want to scare them with your experiences. Your friends might be from your workplace and you might like to keep your home and work lives separate. It can be helpful for you to have a space away from the concerns of home, however, there may also be someone who is going through a similar struggle as you but you're not reaching out to each other. Your family members may not be close to you but may be wanting to help you if only they knew what's going on. Try to be broad in looking at your possible support network and think about how you might be able to test the waters by reaching out and seeing how people respond.

If, after doing this activity you are feeling like there's not enough people around you and your teenager, you might consider seeking out professional support. There are various ways to do this. There are online forums that you can reach out to. Take a look at the list in the resources section and explore the web sites to get a sense of whether they suit you. Your GP might be a useful support but bear in mind that although they are often the first port of call they aren't all experienced with providing support to families and young people who are suicidal. Check to see if there are any GPs in your area who specialise in working with young people. They will most likely have undertaken some additional training and at least will know of some local services who can help you.

Bear in mind that there are at least two sides of the helping equation. You will need some help and support for yourself as a parent to support your teenager but also as a person to keep yourself healthy and coping with your life. Your partner and other family members will also benefit from support. It requires that you reach out and are open to asking for help. It can take time to find the most useful help at any point in time. If you've had a good experience in the past it can be worth revisiting that if possible or identifying what was helpful.

Dealing with feelings of shame and guilt

Right from the moment we learn that we are having a baby we begin, consciously and unconsciously, the process of setting expectations for them, and ourselves as parents. These beliefs or expectations are often reinforced by people around us. For some of us these expectations may have begun to develop early in our life, like in our own childhoods, and certainly well before the pregnancy. These are typically big-picture, high expectations, like I want my child to be happy and healthy. We expect that we will be the best parents, somehow not falling into the traps other parents fall into. It's easy to be critical of others when we're not them of course and while these expectations may have been worthy expectations, or hopes, they are inevitably impossible to achieve. Once we find ourselves at home with the baby we begin to see just how challenging day-to-day survival with a new baby can be. We can start to see the slippage. We start to think about things we never thought about before, particularly related to the safety and wellbeing of the baby. Different expectations of ourselves and others can start to impact as we make assumptions and find others challenging them. Some of us learn to quickly adjust our expectations and find a way to become the good enough parent while others struggle to reconcile the mismatch between our ideal and our reality. Buying into media representations of the perfect parent can add fuel to this challenge. With the advent of social media and images (often very one-sided images) we can increasingly become discontented and feel like we're not able to live up to our or others' expectations. This feeling of not being good enough might be nothing new. Some of us have already held high expectations of ourselves in other areas of our lives, like how we look or what we achieve. In that case, we can just add parenting to the mix of things we wish we could do better.

It's clear then that the groundwork is laid early in our parenting life for us to blame ourselves and take on shame and guilt when things don't go right with our kids. Having a teenager will tap right into these feelings of not being good enough and lead to parents feeling shame and guilt. It's no wonder that parents of teenagers who are suicidal or have suicide attempts will easily blame themselves, and experience shame and embarrassment. This can serve to shut us down and stop us talking to others and even prevent us from reaching out to get help. Overcoming shame can be challenging but talking to other parents in a similar situation can be one of the most helpful ways to reduce these feelings and gain self-acceptance and confidence in our abilities again. It can be helpful to know that feelings of shame and guilt are all about the things that matter to us. They can also be about the expectations of others about what should be done or not done. Shame is often considered to be more about ourselves whereas guilt is about things in the world, such as acts of failures and events that we feel responsibility for. A person who feels guilty regrets something they've done while someone who feels shame regrets something about themselves as a person. Feelings of shame go deeper to a sense of ourselves and our identity. Guilt can more easily be resolved by acting to repair the situation whereas feelings of shame can become personalised and more difficult to shift.

Feelings of shame attached to our teenager's suicidality can tap into earlier times we've felt shame, even as a child or a teenager ourselves. It's helpful for us to recognise this so that we can understand why we may be experiencing strong feelings or experiencing something different to others. We all bring our unique life experiences to our parenting and guilt and shame are examples of how parenting a teenager who is suicidal can trigger our earlier experiences. If we think about parenting a suicidal teenager, there may not be one issue that we feel guilty or shameful about that can easily be fixed. It's more likely that a parent will feel guilty and potentially shameful about their parenting as a whole and the young person will feel guilty and potentially shameful about what they have done. In such cases, expressing these feelings and apologising to each other might open the door to being able to get along together and agreeing to be honest and open. This might take time and may need professional support to help guide the conversation towards one of respect, shared responsibilities and hope for the future.

A good starting point might be to work towards self-forgiveness. A useful workbook is available online written by a clinical psychologist, Professor Everett Worthington (www.forgiveself.com), which can help people work through six steps to forgiveness. The six steps are:

1. Recall an 'offence' — one concrete situation to focus on

2. Repair relationships — make amends with those who have been harmed

3. Rethink rumination — experience the emotional restoration of positive self-regard

4. REACH emotional self-forgiveness — replace self-condemning emotions with positive, growth-oriented emotions

5. Rebuild self-acceptance — being good enough

6. Resolve to live virtuously — connect with values and restoring positive sense of self.

The workbook is a comprehensive tool with a series of exercises for completion for each step. By working your way through the workbook you may be in a better position to manage your own feelings but also to model for your teenager how to do this.

Facing fears

Parents can have many fears about their children's safety and wellbeing. These fears can be real or inflated. Over the course of our lives, and our children's lives, these fears change. From the birth of their children, parents worry about their very survival, feeling the burden, along with the joy, of being totally responsible for them and keeping them alive. As they grow we learn to adjust and what we worried about the year before we may no longer even think about. Those fears will be replaced by new ones as our children's worlds open and they gradually let go of our hold. By the time they are teenagers we might be pretty good at adjusting to these changes, but the world of adolescence opens a whole new range of fears and anxieties that we hadn't dared think about before. Some of those fears might relate to our memories of our own teenage years. Sometimes our fears come from hearing stories, in the media or from other parents who have been there before us. Often the scary stories are told rather than the more calming stories of normal day-to-day life with teenagers. Just as we were primed to feel guilty, we also are primed to feel scared as parents.

When we feel fear, our body and mind respond in ways that can leave us feeling out of control. We might experience panic or a numbing of our thoughts and feelings. We might have a physical response where we feel sick. Our thinking process might slow down and we may not be able to find the words we need. Our vigilant brain might over-think and jump to conclusions that increase our fears, and the cycle begins over again. It can be a debilitating experience and one that can lead to feelings of incompetence. Our fear may push us away from our teenagers. At the very time they need us most, our fear might make us so anxious that we become judgemental or blaming of them. Our fear might make us want to shut down, shut our teenagers away from us, and shut ourselves away from our support networks. Our thoughts and feelings might become silenced as we struggle to contain them, at the very time when we need our thoughts to be clear and our feelings to help us to work out what matters and guide us to prioritising those things.

Being a witness to the struggle of your teenager when experiencing suicidal thoughts and attempts can be frightening and traumatic for parents. Experiencing powerful and recurrent memories of the event and avoiding situations that remind you of the experience can create a cycle of negative thoughts and emotions that might impact on functioning and well-being. It may even lead to symptoms of post-traumatic stress disorder or other anxiety disorders. In the aftermath of a suicide attempt the focus will be on your teenager and it will be easy for your experience to be overlooked, however, it's important not to underestimate the impact of the experience on you. This is particularly the case as parenting a teenager who is suicidal is not a one-off event and the experience for parents doesn't have a clear beginning and end. It may have triggered off a whole lot of fears and worries as you focus on preventing your teenager from hurting themselves again.

The trauma associated with a suicide attempt can relate to the memories of the event and the feelings that accompany the situation, such as guilt. You may also want to protect others from knowing the extent of your experience so you may be trying to deal with your feelings on your own. Your day to day routine may have been shattered as you now face your number one worry about keeping your teenager safe. This can increase the traumatic feelings because you feel isolated and alone. The traumatic experience may be continuing as you struggle with the fear that it will happen again. You may be aware that other family members are also impacted and may see your role as supporting them. Of course, the teenager him or herself may also be impacted and fearful about their suicidal behaviours and you'll be no doubt trying to support them too. Being on edge and over-extending yourself for the immediate period might be necessary to get through a crisis but be mindful of the risk of remaining in this elevated state for a longer period. It will take a toll on your mental and physical health as well as on your social functioning.

When we feel fear, we are likely to become hypervigilant. This creates a physiological impact where we are jumpy and on edge. This state of high energy is not sustainable over time without burning us out. It can mean that we are so worried about our kids that we tend to over-parent — both our teenager that we are worried about but also our other kids. We can start to see things through a narrow lens of risk and worry about things more than we used to — and potentially much more than we need to. We can start to lose perspective of what are real risks and this can have a negative impact on others.

Understanding the way that fear triggers off a physical response can be helpful. If we know that our thoughts of fear and worry can lead to a particular feeling which in turn sets off a particular behaviour, we can begin to focus on reducing the impact of those thoughts. We can try to find ways to give ourselves a break from the fear. This might be by distracting ourselves, even for a few minutes at a time where we give ourselves permission to not think about the worry. We might need to actively turn off the phone for a few minutes or go for a short walk without the mobile phone. It might be with positive self-talk where we tell ourselves that our teenager is okay and we can relax. It may be from sharing our thoughts and gaining support in sharing the responsibility. This necessarily needs to start off with small efforts and build up over time. We can remember that feelings of fear are important because they tell us a lot about what we value and what or who matters most to us. We can't entirely dismiss them, and most likely don't want to, but we can certainly learn to put them into perspective and not let them rule our lives.

Chapter 14

Family relationships

Supporting the entire family unit

While it's necessary to focus on the young person who is suicidal, it is also important to consider the family unit as a whole. Keeping the family unit as strong as possible can be a way to build a strong support network around the young person. Including all the family members in decision making as far as possible, keeping everyone in the loop and finding ways that each family member can contribute will be ways to strengthen family bonds. Recognise that the family's strength will come from being together and supporting each other. Drawing on extended family members and friends can also place a network of supports around the family but take care to prioritise your primary relationships within the family. Taking time out and talking to others can help but ensure that you come back to the family unit to support each other and continue to plan how to deal with the situation.

The parenting relationship(s)

There is not one type of parenting relationship that can be described. Each family has its own structure and dynamics. The situation the family faces when having a teenager who is suicidal is likely to place significant pressure on parents and on the parenting relationship. Equally, the stressful situation can also bring parents together to focus on the needs of the teenager and the family. There are a number of ways that parents can undermine each other however when stressful situations arise, such as blaming each other and sending different messages to the teenager. We often hear about the importance of a united front in parenting and this is important during times of stress. This doesn't mean that parents have to agree on everything and in many ways that is impossible and not always helpful. It can help to hear a different perspective or to consider the situation differently. Having an open discussion in which these perspectives and differences are shared privately will be important and once agreement is made this can then be shared with the teenager. Providing different perspectives or arguing in front of a teenager is likely to create more stress, confusion and even resentment as the teenager can feel like they are not being heard, are given conflicting messages and can feel that the situation is becoming out of control. The teenager can also feel responsible for the arguments and this can lead to a sense of burden, which we've identified earlier as a concern in terms of suicide risk.

Taking time to nurture the parenting relationship and to value it in its own right not just as part of the family unit is important but can be overlooked during times of family stress. This means prioritising time and for parents to make the effort to sit together, listen to each other and plan together how to support each other and the teenager (and other family members). This of course can be challenging if there is existing conflict or parents are separated or divorced but prioritising the teenager's needs can help to focus this attention. Sometimes it may be helpful to work with a professional experienced in couples' relationships to help parents listen and hear each other. Knowing that each parent has a critical role to play with responsibilities as a parent to the teenager who is experiencing distress can help encourage feelings of respect and promote ideas of working together.

Impact on sibling(s): their responses and needs

It's natural that the focus for the family will be on the teenager who has most needs at that time, however, it's also important to consider the impact that this is likely to have on siblings. There are a range of experiences they may have, depending on their age and stage of development, their relationship with the teenager, their own needs at the time and their personality. You will be in a good position to make sense of all of this. It may not be until they begin to 'act out' that you become aware of their needs. This may occur because the family dynamic can shift so that the way of communicating within the family is through risky behaviours.

Ideally you will be able to prevent sibling(s) from feeling like they need to get your attention through risky behaviours by closely monitoring their needs. This can include taking time to spend with them on their own, finding ways to ensure they are able to continue to do the things that are important to them and giving them the chance to talk about their feelings or concerns about what is going on. It is important not to underestimate their own feelings of guilt or shame that may be arising through the experience the family is having with the teenager who is suicidal. Check in with them in relation to any talk that is happening on social media or at school as this can feel like a responsibility for the sibling(s) to carry and they may be concerned about sharing this with you. They may also not want to share their own worries or issues with you because they know you are concerned about their brother or sister. Be clear to make sure you let them know that you are also there for them and don't want them to feel left out or unsupported. This may be a good time to talk with them about who else can be there for them at this time to make sure they have a 'village' of support around them. This could include extended family members or family friends as well as professional help if necessary. Putting in effort to recognise that this is a stressful time for them as well is best done as early as possible, rather than waiting until you see signs that they are not coping.

If siblings do behave in ways that are uncharacteristic, it is important to recognise these behaviours for what they are — as signs that they are needing support. This will require that you firstly listen to them, acknowledge their distress, accept that you may have been focusing on their brother or sister more in recent times and that you can understand how they are feeling. You can then move into a problem-solving approach to work out what needs to be done next. Depending on what they have done, there may be some repair work required. For example, if an incident has happened at the school or there are problems with the police, this will need to be handled with sensitivity. Helping the authorities understand what is happening for the family will be important but there may still be a need for consequences. Including the child or young person in this as much as possible is likely to help. Managing your own emotions, including disappointment (in yourself as well as your child) and stress, will be critical here. Seeing the situation as an opportunity to refocus and read the signs of the whole family in distress can help. This may also be a time when some professional help might be valuable so that you can refocus and decide on priorities. It's likely that you will feel torn between the needs of all family members and this can be challenging. Bear in mind that this won't be the case for ever and the family will shift back to its equilibrium before too long. This can help to get you through the challenging period.

Building resilience and deeper connections

There are ways that families can get through these times and even use the experience to build resilience and deeper connections:

- Focus on what really matters. While it may be tempting to try to take control of things like messy bedrooms, now is not the time to focus on things that don't really matter and may lead to greater disconnection.

- Continue to have high expectations and set boundaries, but do this with support and sensitivity.

- Hold on to important family rituals and routines as far as possible. This helps to build a sense of containment and safety. If necessary, create some new rituals and routines.

- Notice behaviours of each family member, looking for changes and checking out with them how they are feeling. Catching small changes early will help prevent things escalating.

- Protect your adult relationships. This might be with a partner or with other adult family members or friends. Time with adults is important to talk through how to deal with the situation, making sure you are sending consistent messages and providing support to each other.

Seeking and giving support will stop you feeling isolated and alone with the stress.

- Consider seeking professional help. You might do this as an individual, a couple or a family unit. Depending on the support your teenager has, you might need to seek this out or it may become available through the service your teenager is connected to. Talk to each family member about what might be involved. It's unlikely to be useful to force family members to attend, so look for options and encourage everyone to think about it as time to look after themselves.

- Taking into account the ages of siblings, and with respect to your teenager's privacy, provide as much information as you can about what is happening.

- Listen to how siblings are feeling — be ready to acknowledge the mixed emotions and stress they feel as well. Listen particularly to any resentment they may feel.

- After listening, problem solve with them what might help them. Are there things they want you to do with them? Do they also have a worry or need they want to talk about? Who else can help? Do they need some time to themselves? Extended family members and friends may be unsure about how to help. They may not be aware of all the details but are aware of problems happening. This may cause them stress and worry.

- Depending on existing relationships, and again respecting your teenager's privacy, consider how much information you can share.

- Consider whether there are ways they can help. Often extended family members and friends can provide practical support (e.g., meals or transporting other children).

Importance of maintaining and strengthening relationships

Research continues to be very clear that parents and other adults such as extended family members and teachers do indeed have a significant influence on their teenagers, regardless of how it might feel for the adults at times of stress or conflict. There is nothing more important during times of crisis or struggle than focusing on maintaining and strengthening our relationships with our teenagers and within the family more broadly. Finding ways to keep the family unit strong will support you all.

You play an important role in the lives of your teenagers. Teenagers look to you for guidance and support while at the same time gradually gaining independence as they move towards adulthood. Teenagers can benefit from assertive parents who do things like actively monitor their technology use alongside their other behaviours and ways of spending their time. Even when it seems they may not care what you think or want to exclude you from certain areas of their lives it does not mean that you are not important to them — it's just that they are trying to work out where everything fits in their world.

While the parental role is important to teenagers it can be useful to bear in mind that this does not mean that what is valued now is the same as what was valued when the teenager was a child. A child looks to the parent for most things and seeks the parent's approval for things they want to do. Part of adolescent development involves teenagers starting to make decisions for themselves and being less dependent upon their parents. In order to do this they need to practise and start to challenge parents' ideas and requests. It can be really helpful for parents to understand these behaviours as just that — not a personal attack on them or their authority.

Effective and respectful communication continues to be the key to any successful relationship and enables you to pass on your values and to hear what is happening in the life of your teenager — both positive things and any concerns they may have such as bullying. Listening to your teenager can be the single most powerful way to connect with them — this is truly listening by making time to spend together, hearing both the words and the underlying feelings beneath what they are saying and reflecting back what you hear to check that you have heard accurately. By doing this, teenagers get to know that you are really there for them and interested in what they have to say. A by-product of this is that it is also much more likely that teenagers will listen to you if they feel that you listen to them regularly and well. By observing your teenager's behaviour, and drawing on what you know about them already, you will be able to notice when things are worrying them or they are not their usual selves. You can then set up a conversation with them when you say that you have noticed some changes in their behaviour that you are wondering about. It is important to do this in a gentle way that suggests you are curious and interested rather than dominating the conversation or telling the teenager that you know something is wrong with them and expect them to tell you what it is.

Another key aspect of communication involves resolving conflict when it does occur. Conflict can arise for two main reasons: a difference of values exists where you and your teenager see the world differently and place importance on different things; and a conflict of needs when you need different things. When we think about the experiences of young people and the world in which they are growing up it should not really be a surprise that parents and teenagers will have some different values and needs which may result in conflict. We know that teenagers often take on the values of their parents but part of their development can require them to challenge those values and test out new ones.

Common needs of parents relate to safety, respect and managing practicalities such as financial or transport needs. Needs of teenagers might relate to independence and other developmental needs. Reflecting on this and planning ahead of conflict points can be helpful for teenagers to understand what the parents' concerns might be and will be placed in a better position to work with the parent to resolve conflicts. An important part of the relationship is also for parents to listen to teenagers' thoughts about what values and needs are important to them as well. It may be surprising to parents that some of the values and needs will be the same although may play out in practice in some different ways. Finding common ground together is a useful starting point to enable conflicts to be avoided or dealt with effectively.

Spend time together face to face as a family, encourage teenagers to meet up with friends for social events, spend time in the natural world and see technology as one important part of life, but not life itself. Teenagers need a wide range of activities to promote healthy physical, cognitive, social, spiritual and psychological development. Parents influence them through modelling, communicating well and working in partnership to come up with positive ways to spend time together. This will be most successful when parents recognise the many demands on everyone's time, including young people's time. They will have study and work commitments and also want to spend time with their friends. Young people also need sleep and rest time. Remembering that all these commitments are important will help parents plan ahead and be ready to listen to their teenager's needs as well as their own interests in family time together.

Harnessing key parenting skills

If there's ever a time when effective parenting skills are needed it's when parents are supporting a teenager who is suicidal. When working with parents I've often used an activity where I asked them to name all the roles they played as a parent, as if they were advertising for a person to fulfil the parenting role. This usually enabled a rich discussion about the many and various roles that parents fulfil: nurse, financial adviser, nanny, cook, laundry worker, cleaner, teacher, counsellor, decorator, and so on. It's clear from this list that the role of parenting consists of practical tasks as well as emotional and relationship building opportunities. One of my observations was that all parents, regardless of the ages of their kids, listed these roles. Although our work as parents shifts over the years as our kids grow and their needs change, it seems that once we are fulfilling those roles we continue to do so even though they change a bit over the years. It can be hard to negotiate to stop or hand over these roles. It's not as if one day we know that it's the day to stop doing the laundry or that our kids won't need us to be there to listen and support them. Indeed we may be more than happy for some of these roles to continue into their adulthood. Therein lies one of the tensions however as our kids become more independent, wanting to live their own lives, while we may be still seeing ourselves as fulfilling all these roles for them. We may also feel exhausted after doing all this work for so long and send mixed messages to our kids. We may not always clearly communicate what we are actually thinking or feeling.

The more emotional parts of the role are a lot about communication. Listening to kids is one of the key skills that could well be under estimated in parenting. We also have to be assertive at times too and this can be difficult to do well. And then we need to be ready to problem solve when we have some kind of conflict. These are the core communication skills that we need as parents and have formed the basis of many parenting books and programs for decades. Everything we do with our kids as parents, including teaching and guiding them to keep safe and learn, placing boundaries around their behaviours, and encouraging them to take responsibility, relies upon good communication and the more we are aware and confident in our parenting skills the more effective we will be. The good news is that communication skills are all teachable and we can get better with practice.

When young people are suicidal, they will need a balance of care, understanding and support as well as boundaries that will keep them safe. The support will need to be practical and emotional and will vary depending on their age and what they need most. Essentially this is what parenting is all about, and what parents have been doing already, but during times of suicidality everything is magnified and with the heightened safety risks becoming the focus, it's easy to lose sight of what parents know already.

If a young person has identified some underlying issues of concern that can be worked out the suicidal risk might subside quite quickly and the focus of parenting can be on support and understanding to improve the situation and get back into usual routines as much as possible. If, however, the meanings underlying the suicidality are not so evident or there is an underlying mental health issue that hasn't yet been identified, the focus of parenting may need to be as much on safety as on understanding. It is in those circumstances that parents will benefit from professional mental health help, both for the teenager directly, but also to assist the parents in navigating this time.

Chapter 15

Tackling the underlying individual suicide risk factors

A lthough suicidal behaviour can appear to come from nowhere, it's likely that there are a whole range of experiences and concerns that are sitting under the surface for the young person. As we've seen, adolescence is a complex time of life with lots of opportunities but also many challenges. For young people who are suicidal, these challenges may have reached a point where they seem unable to face them, or perhaps one big challenge has led to this situation. The sense of excitement and energy along with hopes and dreams for the future can disappear as the focus narrows down to the here and now. They may have shared some, all or none of their problems with us. While focusing on keeping them safe is important and necessary, we will not be able to help them move beyond their suicidal thoughts and behaviours unless we work with them to handle what is happening for them. This will require us to harness our best parenting skills. Listening, especially, is important, as mentioned throughout this book, but also knowing when and how to be assertive. Our parenting skills may be tested and we may need support to update them to work towards more authoritative ways of parenting.

Mental health problems

When people think about mental health they often jump to the idea of mental health problems or mental illness, so it's important to begin with a definition of good mental health. Mental health is defined by the World Health Organization (2014) as 'a state of wellbeing in which every individual realises his or her own potential, can cope with the normal stresses of life, can work productively and fruitfully, and is able to make a contribution to her or his community'.

A problem with mental health can arise when a young person is experiencing difficulty coping with life or develops signs and symptoms that suggest that there is a problem with their thoughts and feelings. When these begin to impact on a young person over a period of a couple of weeks, across a number of environments and are concerning to them and/or others, we might start to become concerned about an emerging mental health problem. Identifying these signs at an early stage can help to prevent the problem from escalating and becoming more entrenched, at which point it may become a diagnosable mental health disorder. We know that many mental health disorders emerge in adolescence and that the earlier we recognise the signs and act, the better outcomes there will be. It can be difficult to distinguish between normal adolescent behaviours, thoughts and emotions and those that suggest a mental health disorder is emerging. Some ideas for working this out:

- Think about any recent or upcoming events or concerns the young person has been exposed to that could explain the changes. It can be helpful to raise this with your teenager, giving them information about the specific changes you've noticed and gently prompting for anything they are concerned about. It would be normal for example for young people to be feeling a bit more nervous than usual at exam time or to be upset after their friend moves away.

- Are there any possible physical causes that might need checking out by the general practitioner? Hormonal changes, growth spurts or recent illnesses can all place pressure on the developing adolescent body so a physical check-up might identify any underlying physical issues which might be impacting on mental health.

- Is there a family history of mental illness that might be related to the young person's behaviour, thoughts and feelings? Does your teenager's behaviour remind you of anyone in your family? If so, it's worth making an appointment with a psychologist or talking to the GP about a referral to a psychiatrist to explore this further. The earlier any diagnoses are made the better, so that treatment can begin and the effects minimised. Bear in mind that effective treatments are available now for many mental health disorders that may have proven difficult to treat in the past.

- Are school pressures mounting? Sometimes as young people move into the next level of schooling the demands increase. Although we might expect that any difficulties with learning would be identified in primary school, this is not always the case and it may be that these don't become clearly apparent until secondary school. If a young person has a learning disability that hasn't been diagnosed it may be making their school experience challenging. Talking to the teenager about which classes they like and dislike or asking them to show you their homework can be a good start, although it can be difficult for young people to talk about any problems they have with learning. Sometimes their behaviour changes as a way of coping or hiding how hard they are finding the school work. At times young people can have very high expectations of themselves or be perfectionistic and expect that they will be able to perform equally well in each class. This may be creating underlying feelings of failure or frustration that may impact on their ability to learn and affect their mental health.

Sense of self and self-worth

About 20 years ago we were hearing a lot about the importance of self-esteem. I included a topic called 'Building your teenager's self-esteem' in courses I ran with parents of teenagers. Self-esteem related to self-confidence and a feeling of self-satisfaction. A lack of self-esteem was thought to be an underlying problem causing a lot of issues for kids. The solution was thought to be that parents should praise their children and not be too critical. At the time it was a bit like a panacea for parenting. Then some research started to come out that questioned this idea. The research that struck me most revealed that some kids who bullied actually had high self-esteem. Learning about this forced me to question some of the ideas that by that time had been agreed as core to parenting. Self-esteem is still talked about as important and it often surprises me how these ideas can take on a life of their own and are hard to challenge. Having high self-esteem might mean that you are confident in yourself but you might get that confidence from harming others or by over-selling yourself. It might come at the cost of relationships and learning to care about or respect others.

At the same time though we want to be able to respect ourselves and consider ourselves worthy, with rights and responsibilities. Having a strong sense of identity (knowing who we are) and self-worth might be better ways to describe this. These ideas can still be challenged by people as too individualistic, too focused on the individual rather than thinking beyond our individual selves and seeing ourselves in relation to others. This is all very important to consider when teenagers are suicidal. Their sense of who they are and what they stand for can be shattered and lead to a lack of valuing of their lives, which may increase their risk of suicide. Feeling isolated and of no worth to anyone can be factors related to suicide.

Our feelings about ourselves develop over a long period of time and are obviously challenged as people say things about us that are unkind or challenge us. As parents we will have said things to our kids that they may have interpreted in this way. Sometimes giving kids honest feedback or letting them know that we are unhappy with something they've done can cause their sense of self to take a dent. Some kids are more sensitive than others and even feedback given in a gentle way can be taken by some as severe criticism. It can be difficult to know how to teach kids how to behave or learn important life lessons without giving them this kind of feedback. While this is not the time to ruminate about those experiences, it is useful to take some time to reflect on how your teenager might be feeling about themselves:

- What have you heard them say about themselves? Are there patterns? Has this changed recently?

- Have you ever had the sense that they were putting on a confident face when in fact you suspected they weren't very confident at all? When was that?

- Has anyone else ever commented on their self-confidence? What did they say?

- Have you noticed that their behaviours and comments haven't matched at times? What was the situation?

- When have you noticed them looking genuinely proud of themselves? What happened?

Once you have a sense of how your teenager might be feeling about themselves you'll be able to understand them better. You might be tempted to heap them with praise but that's not the answer. Praise that is given for the sake of giving it is not genuine and others see through it or find it condescending. Instead it will be better to find a way to gently open up conversations about what you are noticing and offering to help. Trying to help them claim their own voice and let you know how they are feeling and what they need will be better. If you do feel tempted to praise them (and there will be times when this is appropriate) here are some tips:

- Focus on specifics about what you like and be clear about exactly what they have done (e.g., 'Thanks for taking the food out of your bedroom').

- Be specific about how their behaviour has impacted on you (e.g., 'Now that your room doesn't have any food in it, I can relax and not worry that the house is dirty'). Don't give general praise (e.g., 'You've done a great job').

- Reflect on how their behaviour might positively affect them (e.g., 'Now that your room doesn't have any food in it, you won't have me asking you about it all the time'.)

You'll see that these might just be subtle shifts in how you talk to your teenager but they can make a difference to how they feel about you and your relationship, as well as about themselves. We can fall into the trap of thinking they understand what we are pleased with or not and sometimes when being too general they can miss our point and not understand exactly what we mean.

Helping a young person to recognise their strengths and capacities as well as acknowledging and accepting their limitations can be helpful. Having perfectionistic ideas where the young person thinks they should do everything perfectly can get in the way of feeling worthy. As parents we can be mirrors to our kids, helping them to recognise what it is that makes them unique and ways that they help others. Watching our own self-talk can also help, ensuring that we are modelling self-acceptance and valuing of ourselves as we are. Talking to our teenagers about times when we have made mistakes and how we handled it can be useful. By sharing our own experiences, we are modelling how to do this.

Body image

Body image stands out in the Mission Australia survey as one of the main issues of concern for young people (with 30.4% of respondents in the 2018 survey naming it as an issue of personal concern, with females higher than males) (Carlisle, et. al., 2018). It's another one of those topics that we are yet to fully understand although considerable research is underway. It involves the way in which young people see themselves (related to self-worth and identity) as well as actions that arise from a desire to improve the way they look. It highlights what can happen when the body and mind connect. There's no doubt a role that the media plays in the way that males and females are portrayed, particularly when images are Photoshopped to show unrealistic and impossible body shapes and sizes. This affects both males and females and increasingly younger children are talking about this. This is not surprising when children are seeing these images from a young age and beginning to form ideas about what is valued in our society.

It's important to know that body image might not just be about physical appearance. It also might have something to do with self-control and self-loathing. Controlling the body as a way of feeling better to gain a sense of control when a lot of things are spiraling out of control is one theory. It's incredibly complex and as with other issues it will also need to be explored with the individual directly to fully gain a grasp of what it means at that time for that person. Young people with body image challenges need professional assessment to inform treatment. As with other issues, the earlier this occurs the better the chances of effectively making a difference. When this impacts on eating there is a risk that an eating disorder (such as anorexia nervosa, bulimia, or binge eating disorders) can arise. The risk of suicide is high for people with eating disorders and increasingly funding is being allocated to research and treatments with the aim of reducing it.

Given the complexity then what can parents do to help young people to prevent body image or eating disorder issues or to respond to them?

- Talking about balance and moderation and living a lifestyle where this is modelled is probably helpful as a starting point. One of the challenges with this however is that a person with body image issues, and particularly eating disorders, can have differing perceptions of what is balanced. Arguments about balance and moderation within that context are likely to cause frustration and even risk worsening the situation.

- Exercise may seem like a good thing to do but excessive exercise can become problematic. Much of this can be hidden for some time and this adds to the challenge of tackling it effectively. Careful monitoring of exercise and encouraging a range of activities, including some 'down time' can help.

- Seeking professional advice about any concerning signs you are seeing may be necessary.

Sexuality

When I was growing up parents talked to their kids about the 'bird and bees', a rather unusual euphemism for sex education. In those days, the focus was often on biology and keeping safe from sexually transmitted diseases and avoiding pregnancy. Increasingly, the focus has shifted to also including information about human relationships and the importance of respect in these relationships. While this began to provide a more comprehensive approach to sexuality and human relationships, this still seems way too simplistic compared to what young people need to know about today. We are now much more sophisticated in our understandings of sexuality. We are well aware that not all people will identify as heterosexual and that young people can be homosexual or bisexual. We also know that some children and young people are transgender and there is a growing awareness and acceptance of this in schools and communities. Despite this, pressures on young people who are homosexual, bisexual or transgender or in other ways gender diverse continue to be extreme. These young people are now known to be at a high risk of suicide. Increasingly, there are efforts to include them in research to increase understandings so they can be properly supported.

Talking openly and honestly with teenagers about sexuality and their understandings and encouraging their questions will help young people know that you are prepared to have these conversations. This can be challenging of course and many parents feel uncomfortable about this topic. Recognising that part of adolescent development relates to sexuality will help to remind us that this is important and we can't ignore it. Ensuring they have access to credible and up to date information will be important, particularly if you feel uncomfortable. Being mindful of the way you speak about homosexuality will be important as young people who are homosexual will be looking for signs of how acceptable this will be to share with their parents. Jokes or comments which suggest that you are not approving or can't understand homosexuality will serve to silence teenagers who are identifying as homosexual. This can leave them feeling unloved and disconnected.

Young people also need to be prepared for issues such as 'sexting' which can, like cyberbullying, cause distress. Talking with teenagers about the importance of respecting others as well as themselves will be critical as core values, which can then be translated into online relationships and activities such as sexting. It's also important to know that sexting is common amongst young people as technology use increases and may be seen as normal by teenagers, rather than problematic. Talking to teenagers about when it may become a problem or risks in the future if relationships break down, for example, can help to ensure they are aware of potential risks that they may not have thought about. As with other behaviours, it's important to be non-judgemental if teenagers share their experiences with you. Instead, work with them to understand what happened and work out how to do things differently if necessary in the future.

Alcohol and other drugs

There's been a shift in Australian teenage drinking and other drug use culture in the last few years. The *National Drug Strategy Household Survey* on young people's alcohol and drug use, which is conducted in Australia every two or three years, has shown a reduction in teenagers' use in recent years (2017). There are continuing debates about what has led to this change given that a decade ago there was a lot of concern about teenage binge drinking and experimentation with other substances. For some it seems that young people spending more time on social media has meant that their connections with their peers takes place from the haven of the bedroom rather than connecting over drinking at parties. That's another one of those interesting paradoxes where potential benefits of social media come into play alongside the worries about young people becoming isolated and consumed by technological means of communicating with each other. Another possibility relates to the work of researchers in Australia who, over a decade ago, advocated that parents shouldn't provide alcohol to their teenagers. Prior to that there had been a prevailing belief that parents would be best to have open communication with their kids and even provide a small amount of alcohol so that they knew what their kids were drinking. Of course, and with the benefit that comes with hindsight, we now know that young people often took this further and gratefully took their parents' alcohol but added more alcohol to it. It was a confusing time for parents as young people were given mixed messages about drinking. Gradually around the country, public education supported by laws in some states and territories disallowed parents providing alcohol to teenagers. This set some new ground rules and meant that parents could refer to the laws instead of trying to work it out with their kids. Importantly this provided the opportunities for consistency between parents. This seems to be one of the most significant public education and social change movements that has occurred in recent times. Of course, that's not to say that all young people are now not using alcohol or other drugs and that spending time in bedrooms to communicate with friends is better than socialising in person. It's interesting to explore how things change and what unexpected consequences happen sometimes. Knowing this might empower you to have different kids of conversations with your kids about alcohol and drug use.

There are still risks associated with drinking and substance use that begin in adolescence and continue into adulthood. Alcohol and other drugs can be used for a range of reasons by young people (and adults for that matter) and it's important for adults to understand the circumstances in which the substance use occurs in order to know how to respond. We also have a tendency to demonise illegal drugs, yet alcohol and over-the-counter drugs such as Panadol that are more socially acceptable can cause serious damage to young people. As with many other aspects of parenting, adult modelling comes into play here too. Your response (attitudes and behaviour) to the use of substances will have been observed by your teenagers for their whole life. If they see you using over-the-counter medications in cautious and limited ways they will begin to understand their role and risks. If they see adults drinking alcohol to relax and chill out that can provide a strong message that alcohol helps you do that. An absolute zero tolerance attitude to illegal drugs will mean that young people might not feel like they can discuss this with us. If on the other hand we understand that people use substances for a whole range of purposes, including to test boundaries, to relax, to cope with difficult emotions, to fit into a group, to deal with boredom, to experience life, and so on, we will open the door to being able to understand and not judge people who use substances. We can then have rich and useful discussions.

Drug use can lead to dependency in which case we are best to see it as a medical or mental health issue. As a parent of teenagers, this is difficult territory to navigate. We don't want to feel like we are condoning unsafe substance use yet we need to understand that young people have been and will continue to encounter alcohol and other substances throughout their lives and need us to be guides. As with other aspects of teenage life, some young people will be more attracted to substances than others. Personality and life circumstances play a role here. Some young people will be cautious and not inclined to be affected by their peers as much as others. Experimentation is part of adolescent development and for some young people alcohol and other drugs might be part of this. Walking the line of providing strong messages about safety while leaving the door open for young people to come to us is necessary across all of our parenting, but particularly when it comes to alcohol and other drug use.

The role of alcohol and other drugs is now recognised as a factor that may be related to suicide risk. Using substances can lead to impulsivity and poor decision making which may place young people at increased risk of suicide. The use of some substances can lead to overdose, particularly when illegal substances often have unknown substances and quantities, but even easily accessed medication such as Panadol can be very dangerous and cause significant organ damage or death if taken in excess. It can be difficult to tease out accidental overdoses from suicide attempts. Suicide data in Australia now includes the role of substances and this is becoming an area for further research.

Technology use

While technology is now a key part of our lives, and many aspects of our lives are enhanced by it, it does need careful management by us all. Unlike their parents, young people have grown up with technology and don't know a world without the internet and mobile phones. This means that the way adults see technology won't be the same as the way young people do and this is an important starting point when thinking about how to talk with our kids about managing their technology use. It also means that they will likely be ahead of us in knowing about new technology. Technology can provide access to friends, to entertainment and to learning opportunities. There are some risks that we also need to be aware of and ready to help our kids make sense of, including:

- *Access to content that may not be age-appropriate (e.g., violent or sexual content).* The risk attached to this will vary depending upon the age of our kids, their interest in seeking out this content and factors such as their personality. The younger the teenager the more controls parents need to put in place to reduce the likelihood of access to violent or sexual content. Parents need to become informed about what might be seen online so they can provide guidance and support to help young people make good decisions about how to manage their access to content.

- *Managing time.* Technology can take up a lot of time that takes young people (and ourselves) away from other activities, particularly physical activities and face-to-face social connections. While young people may value spending time on technology it is worth helping them to monitor this. This might need to begin with building awareness of how much time they are spending online. Putting in some boundaries around technology use, particularly for younger teenagers, will be necessary to ensure that young people's lives have balance.

- *Problematic internet use or internet/gaming 'addiction'.* Increasingly this is seen as a potential mental health disorder that needs specific treatment. There are signs that parents can watch out for that could suggest that internet use or gaming is becoming a problem, for example:

  - Spending time on the internet or gaming for longer and longer periods over successive weeks or months

  - Going online as soon as the young person wakes up

  - Neglecting daily routines or responsibilities, such as homework or chores

- Minimising or lying about time spent online when asked by a family member

- Becoming irritable or aggressive when internet usage is curtailed or efforts are made by parents to time-limit software

- Dropping school grades, ability to concentrate in class or not completing homework tasks

- Noticeably declining face-to-face activities, such as sports or hobbies or going out with friends.

When looking at these possible signs, remember that no two young people are the same and their behaviour may vary with some of these signs more apparent than others. In addition some of these signs may not be related to technology use itself but suggestive of other problems. The *Second Australian National Survey on Adolescent Mental Health* conducted in 2014 found that adolescents with major depressive disorder had a higher prevalence of problem internet or gaming behaviour than adolescents with no identified mental disorder. If you notice several of these signs over a period of several weeks or months, it's worth considering the possibility that your teenager is experiencing difficulty managing their technology use and/or could be experiencing difficulties related to a mental health disorder.

- *Cyberbullying and cyber-harassment.* This is the area of concern that we hear most about in relation to suicide risk. Cyberbullying and cyber-harassment involve the use of technology to cause harm to another person through comments, pictures, posts or sharing using emails, mobile phones, social networking sites, chat rooms, web sites and instant messaging programs (basically wherever there can be online contact between people). Like face to face bullying, cyberbullying refers to repeated and deliberate behaviour where there is an abuse of power. The activities can include social exclusion, name-calling, lying or spreading rumours, threats to safety, impersonation, account accessed without consent, personal information posted without consent, and inappropriate or personal pictures posted without consent. It, like face to face bullying, can be psychologically damaging and by its nature pervasive, following the young person home and potentially impacting on them 24 hours a day. Harassment can be a one-off, isolated experience, which can also be damaging to young people.

The Office of the eSafety Commissioner (https://www.esafety.gov.au/) conducts research and provides information and resources for young people and parents. It's worth keeping up to date with the latest information available on their web site and shared via Twitter.

While the earlier list outlines potential harms and risks associated with technology use, it can be useful to remember that technology can also be used to connect with your teenager. Never before have humans been so connected to each other and this can work in your favour. You can show genuine curiosity about how teenagers are engaging with technology and always be ready to learn from them, whether this is a video game, an app they enjoy using or a web site where they are accessing interesting information. This will help your relationship by creating a common reference point, something to talk about and be included in each other's worlds. By finding ways to enter into their world of technology, you are letting them know that you are aware of how important it is to them and the door is opening to you being part of their social world. They can also be in the role of expert as they share information with you. This is important for their sense of self-worth and feelings of competence.

Sleep

Sleep disturbances have been found to be related to increased risk for suicidal symptoms. A study from Stanford University found that sleep problems among young adults at risk for suicide, especially variation in when they went to sleep and when they woke up — emerged as a warning sign of worsening suicidal thoughts in the following days and weeks (Benert, et. al., 2017). They found that falling asleep at very different times each night was especially predictive of an increase in suicidal symptoms. Participants in the study who had a lot of variation in times when they fell asleep also reported more insomnia and nightmares, which also separately predicted more suicidal behaviours. The researchers noted the value of sleep disturbances as a visible warning sign of increased suicide risk. They recognised sleep as a barometer of our wellbeing and directly impacting on how we feel the next day. Poor sleep may fail to provide an emotional respite during times of distress, impacting on the ability to regulate mood, which in turn lowers the threshold for suicidal behaviours. Treating sleep problems is possible and this may in turn assist in reducing suicidal behaviours.

It can sound obvious to say that teenagers need good sleep. Their bodies are growing rapidly and we will know from our own experiences the impact that poor sleep can have on our functioning. Along with healthy diets and exercise, sleep completes the triad of healthy behaviours which promotes positive physical and mental health. There's a lot we can learn about sleep for ourselves and even more about sleep and what it means for teenagers, according to Dr Chris Seton, an Australian adolescent sleep physician. In a chapter about sleep, Understanding Teen Sleep and Drowsy Kids in *Nurturing Young Minds* (Manocha, 2017), he begins with two questions for parents to answer to help decide whether their teenagers are sleep deprived:

1. Does your teenager have big weekend sleep-ins?

2. Are they difficult to wake up and get out of bed on school mornings?

If you answer yes to either or both of these questions, it's likely your teenager is sleep deprived. Both of these behaviours can mean that your teenager is getting insufficient or poor quality sleep and is trying to make up for it. Understanding the effects of sleep deprivation is important in under-standing teenage behaviour and helping to prevent difficulties. Some of these are obvious and are clearly related to sleeping problems, perhaps being direct consequences of poor sleep. However for some, the link with your teenager's current life might not be so obvious. The effects of sleep deprivation can include negative effects on learning, mood disturbances and behavioural problems as well as increased risk of anxiety, depression and suicidal ideation. It's clear then that sleep is critical to your teenager's wellbeing and it may be timely to look at exploring with your teenager how their sleep is going. A visit to the GP is a good first step to begin to address sleeping problems and rule out any other physical issues that might be affecting your teenager.

Chapter 16

Tackling the broader social issues underlying suicide risk

Social relationships, including bullying and relationship break-ups

S ocial relationships are important to young people. Often it's the prospect of being with their friends rather than the excitement of learning that gets them out of bed in the morning and off to school. It's through their social connections that young people can feel like they belong and are important. They are learning to understand themselves and who they are through their interactions and feedback from their peers. They try out different ways of doing things or change the way they look in response to the reactions and views of their peers. Sometimes they find their peer group based on similar interests or other aspects of their lives that they have in common.

While social relationships with peers are critical to adolescent develop-ment, they often create challenges. Sometimes young people can feel pres-sured to do certain things to make friends or to fit into a group. Depending on what is expected this can be problematic. We've often described this as peer pressure and seen it as a negative aspect of fitting in. This experience of fitting in and peer pressure is not that simple. Sometimes young people can be positively influenced by their peers, although we're not as likely to call that peer pressure. Adults can also sound a bit condescending when we talk about peer pressure as an adolescent issue, rather than a factor associated with the need we all might have to fit in and belong to a group or community. To say that peer pressure stops with adolescence is not true, but over time through experience we might become more adept at being aware of when we are feeling pressured and have ways of dealing with it.

When people socialise there can be difficulties in their relationships. Conflicts are pretty normal when people interact. Sometimes people can treat each other inappropriately, saying or doing hurtful things. Depending upon the situation and the harm caused, it might be named as harassment, abuse or bullying. All of these can be damaging and cause long term harm to an individual's mental health, self-confidence, sense of worth and their development. It's interesting to note that research tells us everyone involved in a bullying situation — young people who are both the bully and the target of bullying, and even those who are a witness to bullying — can be affected negatively by the experience. Bullying occurs within the context of social relationships and young people need help to recognise when behaviours or patterns of behaviours are inappropriate and be supported to learn more appropriate ways of responding and to speak up when they feel impacted or they see it happening. Increasingly, cyberbullying has been observed to be particularly damaging to young people because of its intensity and inescapability as young people can access it all day and night. Face to face bullying still occurs however and research suggests that sometimes the young people involved in face to face bullying are also involved in cyberbullying. Parents and teachers can play an important role in helping young people reflect on their relationships, understand what respectful relationships look and feel like and help them to feel confident to assert themselves appropriately. It is important too that adults model respectful relationships and set high expectations about the way young people talk to and about each other. The earlier this is acted upon the less the longer term impact is likely to be. Research has identified links between bullying and increased suicide risk so it's important to look out for signs and encourage young people to talk about their concerns. Knowing there is a range of options to turn to, including reporting to school staff, talking to you and reporting online abuse if necessary will help them feel able to raise concerns.

We will all remember our experiences as adolescents learning about romantic relationships. As Rod Stewart's famous song reminds us, 'the first cut is the deepest' and like other adolescent experiences the first romantic relationships we have will be impactful. One of the warning signs for suicide can be a recent relationship break up so it's important for parents not to minimise the impact of a breakup. Sometimes adults, in attempting to be helpful, can make remarks like 'there are plenty of fish in the sea', 'it's normal, it happens to everyone' or 'you'll have lots more girl or boyfriends before you're ready to settle down so don't worry about it'. These comments dismiss the extent of emotional turmoil a young person could be feeling. A better response is to listen and acknowledge the feelings. Listening will also help you get a better sense of what happened, although of course the young person may not want to share details with you and it's important to respect that. It's also important to remember that, like adult relationships, it may have been complicated and there are likely to be a range of emotions such as embarrassment and jealousy that come with the grief and sadness of the relationship breakup. With social media, there is also the risk that the relationship and the breakup were more public than expected. By offering to help the young person work out how to respond to the situation by firstly working out what the main concerns are and then problem solving together will let them know that you care and are trying to understand.

Knowing someone who has died by suicide

Young people who know someone who has died by suicide are at increased risk of suicide themselves. This is important to know about and it's also important to know that the young person doesn't have to have known the person who died personally or to have been a friend. It can be someone they know of or someone they connect with on some level (e.g., someone who has a similar interest or experience). They can also be affected by celebrity deaths by suicide. Knowing this will help you to check in with your teenager if you become aware that someone they know of has died by suicide. Schools will often alert parents as well and offer support if required.

At times like this it can be important to reach out in a range of ways to your teenager, offering to take them on outings, spending time with them and gently asking how they are going and if they'd like to talk about how they're feeling. If you notice signs of changes such as your teenager becoming more withdrawn, not sleeping, eating differently or becoming more irritable you should talk with them about what you are noticing and offer to get some help for them. Remember that asking them if they are having thoughts of suicide will not put the idea in their head and could rather be the opportunity they need to let you know that they are struggling. If they do share these feelings you can let them know that this is not surprising and you would like to help them. You can ask them if it would help if they talked to you about how they are feeling or if they would like to get some more formal help. Some of the things they may like to talk about is the person who died, how their friends are coping and what they are saying, what the school has done or talked to them about and whether they have any concerns that they would like to share with you. Talking about the person who died can be difficult but it's likely that your teenager might have some ideas about what led to the suicide or may be confused or uncertain about what led to the death. Listening to them as they talk through their thoughts can be really helpful and it's important not to jump to conclusions yourself. Sometimes we can say something that we think is helpful but can be interpreted as judgemental or simplistic. Talk with them about who else might be able to help (e.g., a school wellbeing staff member or psychologist, a mental health professional that you could access through your general practitioner). It's important they have as many contacts as possible. Above all, ensure that they know that you are always ready to listen to how they're feeling and want to be able to help them to manage their feelings. Make sure that your teenager has the Kids Helpline number and other phone numbers available and assure them that you would like them to call these numbers if they feel like they need extra help or you are not immediately available to talk with them.

Family relationships

Family relationships are very much related to suicide prevention and suicide risk. Having cohesive and supportive families are recognised as key to preventing suicide and conflict and disharmony in families are often listed as risk factors. What does this mean within a context of family life with its ever changing tide of emotions and tensions? Of course families will have conflict and disagreements. There are many things that impact on families and if we understand families as a dynamic and changing set of interrelationships we can soon see that it is impossible not to have periods of disharmony. As teenagers look to break away from the family to form their own identity it makes sense that conflicts and debates become part of the tapestry of family life. The question then becomes how does the family unit provide a safe and secure environment in which these tensions and conflicts can play out but a young person still feels valued and heard? I think some of this comes back to parents' own understanding of this adolescent period and not taking conflicts personally. In that way they will model respectful conversations and allow discussions to take place without personalising the argument. If an argument occurs it will be necessary to allow time for everyone to calm down while ensuring that a follow up discussion takes place. This may include an apology or a chance to listen to what hasn't been said or heard. It is the adults that need to lead this and to show the way forward. Young people might well be craving this connection but can't be expected to have the skills and experience it takes to do this. It's not easy and even adult relationships can break down because of an argument that, looking back, didn't seem worth the argument let alone the major, long-term impact it had on the relationship.

The idea of picking your battles can have particular significance for the years of parenting teenagers. Choosing to argue over everything will increase the sense of disharmony; while letting go of things that don't matter in the big picture will enable the important things to be focused on and more weight given to those. Three basic principles can apply to reducing or managing family arguments:

- Pick battles and only risk arguments over things that really matter.

- Ensure that discussions are respectful — learn how to argue well.

- Always come back after an argument when everyone has calmed down to resolve any hurt.

Young people will also be affected by other issues affecting family life, such as the relationship between parents, changing financial circumstances, parents' working life and pressures, and so on. Recognising that these pressures can be noticed by the teenager and lead them to worry can mean that we can be alert to how information is shared and how we model effective coping skills and help seeking.

School and study problems

We've all been to school so we know what it's like. Right? No, not exactly. Everyone will have their own experience of school. Often the buildings and set up seem the same as when we were students. I was often reminded of that as a school psychologist finding my way around secondary schools when I experienced a strong sense of déjà vu from my own school life. The lockers and long corridors with their linoleum floors reminded me of my school days. Although I was a 'good student' valuing and enjoying the opportunity to learn and being compliant (shy really), I often found school a hard place to be. While I found class time to be manageable and even enjoyable because I liked to learn, the navigation of social relationships was difficult for me. As my family moved a lot with my Dad's work I always found myself to be on the outside of, or between, the social groups. I never could work out quite how to make it into the popular groups. I realise now that I often wore a mask of confidence and compliance to manage those years.

Many years later as a school psychologist, students would be referred to me for help with school issues. I always found it helpful to reflect on the way that I put my own mask on during my school years. I could then see my main task as a school psychologist was to work with the student to gently encourage the removal of the mask they wore. For some of them the mask was one of compliance, like mine, but often those kids didn't make the school psychologists' list. Like me they weren't high on the priority when you have others who aren't attending school or are acting out in ways that upset teachers and disrupt the learning of their peers. I was often referred the 'angry boys' and I remember one of my supervisors, who hadn't worked in schools, asking me what was going on in the school to have so many angry kids on my client list. Being angry became the norm for those boys who found school hard. It was better than being seen as not coping. There were also often good reasons why they were angry. Sometimes girls were angry too but more often than not girls tended to withdraw or put on the compliance mask when things weren't going well.

There can be many reasons why young people get angry at school or on the other hand withdraw and refuse to attend school. There can be learning or academic difficulties or pressures. It can be hard to ask for help, even though teachers are often highly attuned to students who might benefit from additional support. Young people can have an average or high IQ but still experience a particular learning difficulty, for example, in maths or language abilities. For others, perfectionist tendencies can place so much pressure on them to do well that they begin to become paralysed with fear and anxiety. To learn new information, we need to take some risks, to be open to entering the unknown, to sit with the 'grey' for a while until gradually we start to make sense of it. This is difficult if you usually pick up on things quickly and don't need help from others to understand. Admitting you don't understand something in front of your peers can be hard for adults, let alone for young people.

As I was well aware as a teenager, school is a complex social environment, where a range of relationships are playing out on a daily basis. In a typical school day a young person will encounter potentially hundreds of other people, depending on the size of their school and how they travel there. I remember travelling to one of my secondary schools on a school bus. This added a whole new layer to my school day. Where would I sit and who would sit next to me? What did it mean if no-one chose to sit next to me? How would I handle the annoying younger kids who made a lot of noise? Could I continue to ignore them or should I say something? How could I impress the older kids? Would we stop at the shop on the way home to get an ice-cream and if so would I have money to spend? How did I make sure at the end of the school day that I made it to the bus in time and didn't miss the bus home? These might seem quite insignificant now as we look back as adults. In many ways the experience equipped me well with the ability to manage the different social interactions and responsibilities you need as an adult. But it was stressful at the time. You may have similar memories. Tapping into those experiences can help us as adults to appreciate the challenges of what looks on the surface to be normal day to day experiences for our kids.

Being connected to school and feeling that school is a safe and supportive environment plays a critical role in student engagement and willingness to attend and commit to learning. Having things dealt with quickly and effectively makes a difference to how young people feel about school. Some of the angry boys I saw as a school psychologist felt aggrieved because a situation hadn't been dealt with fairly. This builds up over time and eats away at the person's sense of who they are and where they fit in, which is important for adolescent development. When we think something has been dealt with unfairly we can behave in various ways — attempt to rectify it ideally but if those efforts are unsuccessful, or we don't have the power, to exert revenge, get pay back or to withdraw completely. Sometimes the hurt that arises from injustice that is left unresolved becomes so damaging that it's difficult to fix later. If important adults in the young person's life don't listen or understand, it can feel helpless, one of the factors associated with suicide risk. If we add a sense of not belonging to the equation, we increase the suicide risk again. Adding a desire to seek revenge can add yet another layer to create a volatile situation. Appreciating the challenges of school life, listening to your teenager and partnering with the school to provide support are the best ways to tackle school challenges.

Chapter 17

Moving forward

Helping young people find meaning in life and hope for the future

There are lots of ways to understand identity and life meaning. This may be contained within cultural and religious beliefs or value systems passed down intergenerationally. They may be spoken or unspoken. Children's identity develops from birth as they see themselves reflected within the relationships with those around them. Humans are social beings and while we value individuality in western culture we develop our understandings of ourselves and others through the social relationships and modelling we receive from childhood. It is within that context that life meaning or purpose develops. According to the United States-based *Six Seconds* CEO, Josh Freedman, (www.6seconds.org), life meaning and purpose occur within a context of motivation, optimism and goalsetting. When these three competencies are present, young people will feel a fire inside, see possibilities, and want to contribute to the world. This leads to a connection with internal efficacy, that inner sense that they are capable and can achieve what they set out to achieve. The influence of families can mean different things depending on the age of the child or young person. Some children and young people are more obviously influenced by their family. However, all young people are likely to go through a phase of rejecting this influence. This questioning of the family's beliefs and values is important during adolescence and is connected to the young person's growing independence and sense of identity. Finding ways to open up discussions with your teenager about the meaning of life can be critical to help make sense of their current experiences and begin to see hope and to see the point of planning for the future. You may have ways that work for you already but it's likely at times when a young person is feeling suicidal that you may also need to find some new ways to open up conversations around topics you haven't talked about before or when discussions haven't gone well. Coming from a 'genuine curiosity' stance can be useful rather than a 'having all the answers' stance. Using television or social media news stories can help to open the conversation safely. Some ways to open up discussions are:

1. Instead of 'I don't like … or I think…', ask 'Do you like …?' or 'What do you think about …?'.

2. 'I'm interested in what it's like for people your age these days to …'.

3. 'I'm not sure about that … what do you think?'.

4. 'I don't really understand what that means. Can you explain it?'.

5. 'This seems really complicated to make sense of. Is there any way I can help?'.

6. 'When you've got some time I'd love if you could explain that to me'.

7. Instead of 'When I was your age' …, say 'This is so different to when I was your age. I can't really imagine what it's like for you' or 'This sounds similar to when I was your age but I wonder if it is'.

8. 'Do you think much about what you'll be doing in a couple of years' time?'.

9. 'What's the best way I can help you?'.

10. 'I heard about … and I was wondering whether that might be happening for you?'.

Facing the possibility of suicide in someone close to us can lead us to question the meaning of life. We might already do this regularly, but thinking about a child or young person who is feeling such distress that makes life not worth living can lead us to question in a way that we may not ever have questioned before. Helping others to find meaning in life can be incredibly confronting but it's pretty important for us to take the perspective of our young person when both trying to understand their distress but also to help them to overcome the feelings of suicidality. Overcoming suicidal thoughts requires a belief that:

- things can and will improve
- the difficult things that are happening at the moment will stop
- they will be able to handle what is ahead, and
- it will be worth it.

As parents we might feel like we know these things will happen but telling our kids that won't be enough. In fact telling them this without encouraging them to share their thoughts could be experienced by them as dismissive and unhelpful. Our job then will be to help find ways for these to become real. We can best help a young person to work this out for themselves by truly listening and helping them come to their own awareness and recognition of what can be. If they tell us that something is wrong, we will help them best by listening and believing them. We can problem solve with them about how to resolve the situation once it becomes tangible. This is not the time to take over but to be with them, walking alongside them, taking their lead as much as possible.

We can ask ourselves questions that can help us to think about what might be useful to prompt them:

- How would you describe their personality?
- What makes them different to other people their age?
- What interests have they held for a long time?
- When does time pass quickly for them?
- When are they happiest? What are they doing? How can you tell?
- When do their eyes sparkle? What are they talking about or doing?

- How do you imagine them as young adults? How might this match their own ideas?

- What words do you use when describing them to your friends or family members?

- What hints have they given you about what they want to do as an adult?

Dealing with the present while looking forward

I recall a period in my life as an adult when I became unwell with Bell's palsy. Bell's palsy is a pretty nasty ailment. Basically, without warning you wake in the morning with one side of your face drooping. Your eye won't shut and one side of your mouth sags. Efforts to shut your eye hurt and attempts to drink your morning coffee result in dribbling. When I realised what was happening I was sure there was something seriously wrong like I'd had a stroke. A visit to the doctor confirmed thankfully that it was Bell's palsy, a debilitating but temporary condition, particularly once you begin with steroids. A patch was prescribed to cover my eye. I struggled to eat and refused to leave the house for several weeks. I felt lightheaded and nauseous. The steroids hurt my stomach and on one occasion I was forced to leave the house to have an ultrasound to check that nothing else was going on. I felt embarrassed with my drooping face and felt terribly unwell. It seemed that my world had suddenly closed in around me. My usual routines ceased. Bedbound to avoid falling over when I tried to walk, I slept for days. Efforts to read or watch television made me feel worse. I felt helpless and worried that my life would never be the same again. I remember thinking that this time would never end with the 'groundhog day' feeling of surviving, doing only what was absolutely necessary to get through. I hated being dependent on others to help me do the basic things to keep the family functioning. Thankfully this terrible period did end and gradually I recovered.

I often look back on that experience as a time that I learned so much about myself and what I thought was most important. I learned to accept support from friends and family. I let go of things that didn't really matter. I learned to value some of the things I'd previously taken for granted and to appreciate what I have. Going to the market for example on a Saturday morning or simply being able to read a book. I've often drawn on that experience since to remind myself that it helps to deal with difficult times by focusing on one day at a time, and on some days focusing on each hour or even worrying about life minute by minute to avoid becoming totally over-whelmed. Getting too far ahead of ourselves doesn't help, yet at the same time it's critical to be able to find a way to hold on to the ability to look forward to the day when things will be better. Sitting with the uncertainty of this can be difficult, not knowing what will happen, not feeling confident in our abilities to know what to do. Allowing ourselves to tune into doing what we think is best at the time is all part of this uncertainty. Accepting what we can't change and refocusing on what we can do something about can help us to remain positive and set realistic goals, the smaller and more tangible the better.

If you reflect on a time of stress in your own life you might recall the feeling of being stuck. You may have little recollection of specific details of that time. You may have put aspects of your life on hold while you priori-tised what were the most important parts of your life at that moment. Both your physical and mental health may have been affected. Relationships might have been enhanced or diminished. You may have discovered things about yourself that you didn't know until then. You may have realised that there are some things that you can't control or are out of reach. Some things that had seemed critically important may suddenly have lost their impor-tance. On looking back, like me, you may have recognised strengths and capacities you didn't know you had. Until we are tested, we don't really know what our capacities might be.

These past experiences can be very helpful to draw upon when going through a period of stress with a teenager who is suicidal. Knowing that there are some things that you can control and some things you can't will be helpful. Prioritising what is the most important thing at that time will be critical. At its most basic, this may well be helping your teenager to stay alive. It can help to know that while we need to focus on what is most important in the present, we also need to look toward the future with hope and energy. We need to believe, and help our teenager believe, that we can get through this period, that despite what it feels like now it won't always be like this.

Being there when times get tough

When we are confronted by frightening things, humans tend to respond in one of three ways — fight, flight or freeze. This is related to our survival instincts from the days when our ancestors were chased by wild animals. I always have an image of being chased by a huge bear when I think about this response. Perhaps that was an example one of my psychology lecturers gave when describing this experience. It sticks well in my mind, because I can imagine myself having any one or all of the three responses if confronted by a bear in a forest. While I might want to fight back with a big stick, I might equally feel the desire to flee and can also imagine being frozen and stuck on the spot. I've also had these experiences when confronted with nonbear-like experiences, such as presenting to a large audience. I've had to resist the urge to flee on a few occasions. I've also had the experience of my mouth becoming so dry it wouldn't open properly, like my tongue is stuck to the roof of my mouth. I prefer to engage the fight response instead, not in an aggressive way towards the audience, but rather through breathing and harnessing my inner strength through self-talk. A few nervous butterflies can trigger a better performance than if I'm too calm and confident. It helps to remind myself of how normal these feelings are.

So what does this have to do with supporting our teenagers at difficult times? We may feel any or all of these experiences when confronted with the worry of our teenager. Let's look at each of these in turn:

1. *Fight.* At times we may have the urge to fight, to argue with the teenager or with professionals trying to help. If this is attacking or blaming it will be unhelpful and is likely to exacerbate the situation. If, however, we harness the urge to fight to build confidence and create an environment of hope it can be helpful.

2. *Flight.* We might find it all too difficult and want to avoid the situation. Again this can be unhelpful, such as times when we disconnect or make ourselves unavailable. If we flee through the unhealthy use of substances or other escapes that can be harmful if used excessively, we will create a range of new problems for ourselves. However, recognising the urge as a need to take some time out and having a break to calm ourselves might be a useful strategy that allows us to be there for the long haul. We need breaks and time to reflect

and re-focus to maintain ourselves. If we plan this carefully and bring in supports if necessary as back up we can make good use of this.

3. *Freeze.* Feeling incapacitated and uncertain is a common experience for people in stressful situations. This can lead to a feeling of panic and distress, a sense that we are out of control and not coping. Knowing that this is a normal reaction can be helpful to us to recognise that it will be temporary. Seeing this as a chance to stop and slow down, to restock our energy and even let others help can be a useful reframing of this situation. It can stop us rushing into a situation and making it worse. It can give others the chance to step up and help us.

Learning ways to manage these experiences will be helpful too. Typically self-talk as we tell ourselves this is a normal reaction as well as breathing exercises can be simple ways of managing these times. When teenagers are feeling suicidal, they need people around them who are able to sit with their distressed feelings, helping them work out what can make things better and feel hopeful about the future. Being a consistent support who will be there will let the young person know what they can do and listening to the young person as they try to make sense of the situation will be important. Sometimes being there and sitting in silence can be the most useful thing to do. These are the basic human skills we've talked about a lot throughout this book. Young people can be supported to explore options without the feeling of being pressured into a particular decision. Trying to explain away feelings or dismiss the strength of feelings will be unhelpful. Listening and accepting the young person is important. It doesn't matter whether you agree with everything the young person says. The most important aspect of the current situation will be that they feel supported and hopeful. Without that they can remain struck and not able to see how things can improve in the future.

Planning to get through tough times

The young person should have a safety plan that will outline the role of parents but parents will also need to have a broader plan to support the young person, including managing their own ability to cope with this situation over a significant period of time. Suicidal behaviour takes time to resolve and parents will usually be there for the long haul. When planning ahead, it is essential to consider 'what can be done' and 'who can help' (see the Table 17.1).

When planning ahead, there are different types of plans to consider. These will range in seriousness from periods of crisis, when your teenager is feeling suicidal or actively hurting him or herself, to longer term plans where you are helping your teenager plan for the future. It can be useful to think about crisis planning as short term and related to a particular situation but still also connected to the other plans. The crisis can be difficult but having plans in place to work towards reducing or eliminating these periods over time is necessary in order to continue to plan for the future. Being prepared can also help to reduce the impact of the crisis. Much of this book has focused on the point of crisis and it can be useful to also think about longer term plans.

Reflecting on what happened after a crisis passes and what can be learned from it can be built into other plans. If we only plan for the future without thinking about the current situation and facing the reality that we might face crises from time to time we can feel like our longer term plans aren't achievable. By holding onto the reality that crisis planning is something we all need to be prepared for while also planning for future goals, we can be better prepared and not let our longer term plans be pushed off track if a crisis occurs. If we only focus on the crisis without longer term planning, we can become bogged down and stuck. Hopes and dreams can form part of the longer term plans and help to shift the focus away from the here and now of the crisis.

Medium term plans for young people might include a focus on finishing school, connecting with friends and family and spending time with hobbies and interests. Helping young people to identify how they want to spend their time will help them to make choices about what will help them to keep safe, build their confidence and help them feel like their life has meaning. Listening to their ideas without judgement will be important so that they feel like the plan is their own. You can add suggestions or ideas for consideration but make sure, as far as possible, it is your teenager's plan and not yours. There are many ways to set up plans:

- Look at a calendar for the next few months. Plot out any significant dates — birthdays, holidays, school events, and so on.

Table 17.1 Planning Considerations

Considerations	What can be done?	Who can help?
Clarity about the Safety Plan and the parents' role in it		
Supporting the young person to see mental health professionals — transport, cost, time		
Accessing mental health support for parents and other family members		
Having phone numbers and a clear plan in case of escalation, available for all family members to be aware of and agreed with the young person. Make sure it's visible (e.g., on mobile phones or posted on the fridge)		
Making time to spend as a whole family together — routines, celebrations		
Making time to build family relationships — special time for parents, special time for parents with each child		
Making time for family members to have time for themselves, e.g. for hobbies and interests, or to relax		
Developing strategies with the school to identify any concerns at the first possible time — identifying a key contact person and finding a suitable way to communicate, building in confidentiality.		
Planning what information should be shared with extended family members and friends		

- Identify key goals and develop a plan to achieve the goals; for example, for a sporting goal, plot back to include training goals. The same can apply to school or study tasks. Setting key dates with realistic expectations can help to make tasks seem manageable.

- To achieve some goals, research might be required. This may include research on the web or through reading books but could also include talking to people who have experience or knowledge in the area of interest. This can be built into the plan as well.

- If a goal costs money, developing a saving plan might be needed. This might require budgeting and will need to take into account ways of earning money or managing pocket money, depending on your teenager's current situation. Being realistic is important and balancing work with study commitments will be important as well.

Longer term plans might focus on future plans for study, and/or work or travel. Holding a meaningful goal in mind can be helpful to keep focused on the reasons for living — and for keeping safe in the here and now. The more concrete the steps in planning the better. Regularly reviewing and adjusting is important so that the plans can both feel like they are within reach and can be achievable. Sometimes the timeframe might need to shift or the goals might need to be broken down even further. That is all part of goal setting and monitoring and shouldn't be seen as failure. Sometimes over time the goal may change or not be a priority any more. In many ways that's not what's important. The process of planning implies hope for the future and the prospect of things being better and manageable. There are many ways to set up a plan for the longer term. Bear in mind that young people are often very focused on the here and now and may benefit from support to see the links between actions now and future goals. A year or two can seem like a very long time for a young person. For further information about goal setting see Reachout.com How to set goals (see reachout.com).

Conclusion

While having a teenager who is suicidal can be confronting and frightening, this book has outlined the many ways that parents can understand their teenagers' needs and work towards supporting them. While death by suicide is a rare event, it does happen and it's important that parents take any concerns about suicide seriously. Knowing what to do and feeling confident in their abilities to do this will help parents feel confident to take action and show their teenagers that they are able and willing to help. Adolescence is a busy time and it's impossible to think about any one aspect of the teenagers' life, including suicidality, without an understanding of all the things that are going on for them. The very nature of adolescence means that we may be excluded from some of these things as teenagers reach for independence from their parents. Having others in the extended family and friendship circle who are available to provide support can help but sometimes professional help will be required. Sometimes the teenager will be reluctant to seek professional help and it can still be helpful for the parents to seek help for themselves. Professional help can provide a safe space to share concerns and consider how to respond to challenging situations.

During times of crisis or stress, small things can make a difference and this may be the focus as much as making major changes. Although there's still much to learn about suicidality and adolescent behaviours, we know enough about the importance of effective communication and the value of strong and trusting relationships to be able to act on those to improve the family situation. Knowing that there are enough parents experiencing their teenagers' suicidality that this book has been written will help parents feel less alone and isolated in their struggles. Historically, adolescence has brought challenges to parenting. It really does come with the territory and hopefully this book has made it clearer just why these challenges occur. Having said that however it is possible to have a good overall relationship between parents and their teenagers, where tension and conflicts might occur, but there is an underlying knowledge that parents care about their kids and will be there for them. Being there to listen and problem solve sound too simple for complex problems but they can be the very things that kids need when they're struggling.

Bibliography and further reading

Introduction

13 Reasons Why. Netflix series (2017). Available from
https://www.netflix.com/au/title/80117470

Asher, J. (2007). *13 reasons why*. London, England: Penguin Books.

Australian Bureau of Statistics. (2017). *Causes of death, Australia, 2017.
Intentional self-harm, key characteristics.* Available from
https://www.abs.gov.au/ausstats/abs@.nsf/Lookup/by%20Subject/3303.0~201
7~Main%20Features~Intentional%20self-harm,%20key%20characteristics~3

Douglas, A. (2017). Parenting through the storm. New York, NY: Guilford Press.

Northwestern School of Communication. (2018). *Exploring how parents and
teens responded to 13 Reasons Why*. Australia and New Zealand. Available
from https://13reasonsresearch.soc.northwestern.edu/netflix_anz-
report_final-print.pdf

O'Grady, L. (2008). *The world of adolescence. Using photovoice to explore psychological sense of community and wellbeing in adolescents with and without an
intellectual disability* (Thesis, Victoria University, Australia). Available from
https://core.ac.uk/download/pdf/10827176.pdf

Chapter 1

Baumrind D. (1966). Effects of authoritative parental control on child behavior. *Child Development, 37*(4), 887–907.

Bowlby, J. (2005). *A secure base.* New York, NY: Routledge Classics.

Karen, R. (1994). *Becoming attached. First relationships and how they shape our capacity to love.* New York, NY: Oxford University Press.

McConnell, M. & Moss, E. (2011). Attachment across the life span: Factors that contribute to stability and change. *Australian Journal of Educational and Developmental Psychology,* 11, 60–77.

Siegal, D.J. & Hartzell, M. (2014). *Parenting from the inside out. How a deeper self-understanding can help you raise children who thrive.* London, England: Penguin. (Particularly Chapters 5 and Chapter 6).

Wake, A. (2012). *The good enough Parent: How to provide for your child's social and emotional development.* Melbourne, Victoria: Palmer Higgs.

Winnicott, D.W. (1987). *The child, the family and the outside world.* New York, NY: Perseus.

Chapter 2

Crawford, M. & Rossiter, G. (2006). *Reasons for living. Education and young people's search for meaning, identity and spirituality. A Handbook.* Camberwell, Victoria: ACER Press.

Erikson, E.H. (1968). *Identity. Youth and crisis.* New York, NY: Wiley.

Mission Australia Youth Survey Report (2018). Available from https://www.missionaustralia.com.au/publications/youth-survey

O'Grady, L. (2008). The world of adolescence. Using photovoice to explore psychological sense of community and wellbeing in adolescents with and without an intellectual disability (Thesis, Victoria University, Australia). Available from https://core.ac.uk/download/pdf/10827176.pdf

Prensky, M. (2001). Digital natives, digital immigrants, on the horizon. *MCB University Press,* 9, 5.

Siegel, D. (2013). Brainstorm: The power and purpose of the teenage brain. New York, NY: Penguin.

Chapter 3

Elgar, F.J., Napoletano, A., Saul, G., Dirks, M.A., Craig, W., Poteat, V.P., … Koenig B.W. (2014). Cyberbullying victimization and mental health in adolescents and the moderating role of family dinners. *JAAMA Pediatrics,* *68*(11):1015–1022. doi: 10.1001/jamapediatrics.2014.1223

Chapter 4

Dunkley, C., Borthwick, A., Bartlett, R., Dunkley, L., Palmer, S., Gleeson, S., & Kingdon, D. (2018). Hearing the suicidal patient's emotional pain. A typological model to improve communication, *Crisis, 39*(4), 267–274.

Durkheim, E. (1987). *Suicide. A study in sociology.* Routledge.

Hawton, K., Saunders, K., & O'Connor, R. (2012). Self-harm and suicide in adolescents. *The Lancet, 379*(9834), 2373–2382. doi: 10.1016/S0140-6736(12)60322-5

Joiner, T. (2005). *Why people die by suicide.* Cambridge, MA: Harvard University Press.

O'Connor, R.C., & Kirtley, O.J. (2018). The integrated motivational–volitional model of suicidal behaviour. *Philosophical Transactions of the Royal Society London B, Biological Sciences, 373.* doi: 10.1098/rstb.2017.0268

Shneidman, E.S. (1993). Suicide as psychache, Commentary. *The Journal of Nervous and Mental Disease, 181*(3), 145–147.

Wasserman, D. & Wasserman, C. (Eds.). (2012). *Oxford Textbook of Suicidology and Suicide Prevention: A Global Perspective.* New York, NY: Oxford University Press.

yourtown. (2018). *Kids Helpline Insights 2017. National Statistical Overview.* Brisbane, Queensland: Author. Retrieved from https://www.yourtown.com.au/sites/default/files/document/2017%20KHL%20Insights%20Report%20-%20Statistical%20Overview.pdf

Chapter 5

Risk and Protective Factors Life in Mind Australia. Available from https://www.lifeinmindaustralia.com.au/about-suicide/risk-and-protective-factors

Jones J.D., Boyd, R C., Calkins, M.E., Ahmed, A., Moore, T.M., Barzilay, R., Benton, T.D., & Gur, R.E. (2019). Parent-Adolescent Agreement About Adolescents' Suicidal Thoughts. *Pediatrics,* e20181771,

Van Heeringen, K. (2012). Stress–Diathesis Model of Suicidal Behavior. In Y. Dwivedi, (Ed.) *The Neurological Basis of Suicide.* Boca Raton (FL):CRC Press/Taylor & Francis.

Chapter 6

Australian Bureau of Statistics. (2019). Causes of Death, Australia 2018: Intentional Self-Harm: Key characteristics. Available from: https://www.abs.gov.au/ausstats/abs@.nsf/Lookup/by%20Subject/3303.0~2018~Main%20Features~Intentional%20self-harm,%20key%20characteristics~3

Colorado Office of the Attorney General. (2018). *Community conversations to inform youth suicide prevention: A study of youth suicide in four Colorado counties.* Available from https://coag.gov/sites/default/files/final_youth_suicide_in_colorado_report_10.01.18.pdf

Mitchell, P. (2000). *Valuing Young Lives. Evaluation of the National Youth Suicide Prevention Strategy.* Australian Institute of Family Studies.

Pearson, C. (2019, January 15). Half of parents whose teens consider suicide have no idea. *Huffington Post.* Available from https://www.huffingtonpost.com.au/entry/parents-teens-suicide_n_5c38dfc4e4b0e0baf53d3748

Robinson, J., Bailey, E., Browne, V., Cox, G., & Hooper, C. (2016). *Raising the bar for youth suicide prevention.* Melbourne, Victoria: Orygen, The National Centre of Excellence in Youth Mental Health. Available from https://www.orygen.org.au/Policy-Advocacy/Policy-Reports/Raising-the-bar-for-youth-suicide-prevention/orygen-Suicide-Prevention-Policy-Report.aspx?ext

yourtown. (2017). *Preventing suicide: The voice of children and young people. Insights Part 2. Young people's experience: What helps and what doesn't.* Brisbane, Queensland: Author.

Chapter 7

13 Reasons Why. Netflix series (2017). Available from https://www.netflix.com/au/title/80117470.

Freuchen, A., Ulland, D., & Mesel, T. (2018). Suicide notes written by child and adolescent suicide victims: A qualitative textual analysis. *Scandinavian Psychologist, 5,* e9.

Lezine, D.A. (2008). *Eight stories up: An adolescent chooses hope over suicide.* New York, NY: Oxford University Press.

Chapter 8

Buus, N., Caspersen, J., Hansen, R., Stenager, E., & Fleischer, E. (2014). Experiences of parents whose sons or daughters have (had) attempted suicide. *Journal of advanced nursing, 70*(4), 823–832.

Torraville, M.A. (2000). Adolescent suicidal behaviours: a phenomenological study of mothers' experiences (Doctoral dissertation, Memorial University of Newfoundland).

Chapter 9

Freedenthal, S. (2017). *Helping the suicidal person.* New York, NY: Routledge.

Chapter 10

Beyondblue Beyond Now Safety Planning App: https://www.beyondblue.org.au/get-support/beyondnow-suicide-safety-planning

Chapter 12

Friedman, R.A. (2014). Antidepressants' black box warning — 10 years on. *New England Journal of Medicine, 371*, 1666–1668. Available from https://www.nejm.org/doi/full/10.1056/NEJMp1408480

Robinson, J., Bailey, E., Witt, K., Stafanac, N., Milner, A., Currier, D., … Hetrick. S. (2018). What works in youth suicide prevention? A systematic review and meta-analysis. *EClinical Medicine, 4–5*, 52–91. Available from https://www.thelancet.com/action/showPdf?pii=S2589-5370%2818%2930041-5

Wasserman, D., Hoven, C.W., Wasserman C., Wall M., Eisenberg R., Hadlaczky G., et al. (2015). School-based suicide prevention programmes: the SEYLE cluster-randomised, controlled trial. *Lancet.* 18;385(9977):1536-44.

Chapter 13

Sanderson, C. (2015). *Counselling skills for working with shame.* London, England: Jessica Kingsley.

Chapter 14

Gordon, T. (2000). *Parent effectiveness training.* New York, NY: Random House.

Chapter 15 and Chapter 16

Australian Institute of Health and Welfare. (2017). *National Drug Strategy Household Survey 2016: Detailed findings*. Drug Statistics Series No. 31. Cat. No. PHE 214. Canberra, Australia: Author.

Bernert R.A., Hom, M.A., Iwata, N.G., & Joiner, T.E (2017). Objectively Assessed Sleep Variability as an Acute Warning Sign of Suicidal Ideation in a Longitudinal Evaluation of Young Adults at High Suicide Risk. *Journal of Clinical Psychiatry*. 78(6): e678-e687.

Carlisle, E., Fildes, J., Hall, S., Hicking, V., Perrens, B. and Plummer, J. (2018). *Youth Survey Report 2018*, Mission Australia.

Lawrence, D., Johnson, S., Hafekost, J., Boterhoven De Haan, K., Sawyer, M., Ainley, J., Zubrick, S.R. (2015). *The mental health of children and adolescents. Report on the second Australian Child and Adolescent Survey of Mental Health and Wellbeing*. Canberra, Australia: Department of Health. Available from http://www.health.gov.au/internet/main/publishing.nsf/Content/mental-pubs-m-child2

Seton, C. (2017). Understanding Teen Sleep and Drowsy Kids. In R. Manocha (Ed.). *Nurturing young minds*. Sydney: Hachette Australia.

Manocha, R. (Ed.) (2017). *Growing happy, healthy young minds*. Sydney, Hachette Australia.

World Health Organization. (2014). *Mental Health: A state of wellbeing*. Available from: https://www.who.int/features/factfiles/mental_health/en/

What to do if your child is not yet a teenager

If you are a parent of a child who is not yet a teenager you may find that some of the information in this book is useful but because of the focus on adolescence there may be some aspects of the book that are not relevant to your child at the moment. The sections on how you might feel and what to do to help your child will be relevant, particularly seeking help and working with the school.

There are some additional important points that are important for you to know about when a younger child is talking about suicide or acting on suicidal thoughts:

- Regardless of the age of your child, it is important to take seriously any talk or acts related to suicide. Children can and do die from suicide, although thankfully it is a rare event.

- Young children can develop plans for suicide and can act on these. Sometimes these acts might not look like suicide attempts so you will need to be alert to actions that may suggest that your child is trying to hurt themselves. They might, for example, use what they have available like skipping ropes or belts, jump from buildings (not necessarily from a height) and run on roads or railway tracks.

- Children are particularly sensitive to whatever is happening in the family and things like family changes and conflict have been identified as some of the factors related to suicide in children. Some of these can be difficult to avoid (such as moving house or schools) but it is important that parents learn to see the world from their child's perspective. Remembering also that each child will see the world differently and respond to situations in different ways is also important in not dismissing their experiences. Gaining a sense of what is happening at school is also important, as there is some research in relation to suicide in childhood that suggests that getting into trouble at school or struggling with learning can be related to suicide risk.

- You will be able to supervise your child more easily than parents can supervise older children so make sure that you, or other adults, are monitoring the child's behaviour and keeping a close eye on them. This needs to be carefully managed so that the child can continue to make their own age-appropriate decisions as well, so be creative in ways you monitor closely without restricting your child too much.

- Knowing that your child has suicidal thoughts or plans can be confronting but you are in a good position to be able to help them. Ignoring or minimising their feelings or criticising or punishing the child will not be helpful as they can learn to hide these feelings and the suicidal acts can re-emerge later on.

- Spending time talking with the child, your child's teacher and other adults and family members will be useful to try to understand what the child's suicidal thoughts and actions mean. Trying to remain calm while taking a curiosity stance will be most helpful. Getting professional help to work this through will be very helpful as you may not be able to see some of the important things that are happening in your family that may be causing stress for your child.

- There is much we can do to help children learn to express their feelings and cope when things are difficult. Schools are increasingly including this kind of education in their curriculum (social and emotional learning) and parents can support this at home so that children get clear and consistent messages. These are some of the skills that will equip them to deal with challenges and be more able to ask for help if they need it.

What to do if your child is a young adult

Much of what has been included in this book will be relevant to parents of young adults. Some aspects will depend on whether your child lives with you or lives independently. If he or she lives independently, you won't have the same level of contact as you will for those who live at home. They may also have more of their own support network around them so your role as parent might be less clear cut. There may be aspects of their lives that you really have no idea about. It will be harder to keep track of them and know where they are and if they are safe. This may mean you feel more concerned about their safety and wellbeing. Here are some ideas to take all of these into account:

- There will be a lot of life experiences that your young adult has that you are not part of or won't know about. This can be challenging when we are concerned about them but important from a developmental point of view. It also means that current family factors may be less related to any suicide risk compared to teenagers. That's not to say, however, that there's not any connection with family or that families don't matter to young adults. This is a time to renegotiate what it means to be part of your family.

- Be clear that you are wanting to be there for them, while also acknowledging their independence.

- Be open to other supports they have (e.g., friends) and check in with them about who they are in contact with and who know about their current situation. You might be able to help them to decide who to tell and how to share relevant information to set up a useful support network around them.

- Make a plan with them about how to keep in contact in ways that work for you both. This might include a regular phone check in or visit. Again, keeping the balance between your caring and wanting to be there for them while respecting independence will be important.

- Ask them how they would like you to help them or how you can be most helpful during challenging times. This might include practical things like cooking or simply spending time with them. Depending on circumstances you might offer for them to stay with you or for you to stay with them. Open up all possibilities and be ready to help but remember that they will want to be independent and not feel like you are treating them as a child. Be prepared also for a situation where they do want your support and their response is more like a teenager. This can occur when people are distressed and finding it hard to cope (like they may have regressed in their behaviours when a child).

- As part of safety planning, arrange how you will stay in touch and discuss what you can do if you are concerned. Having the conversation and gaining agreement beforehand can help avoid confusion or conflict later.

- Seek support for yourself. Recognise that there will be times when you will feel uncertain and potentially out of control of the situation as your child seeks out their own way of dealing with their situation.

Useful resources

There are a number of evidence-based parenting programs in Australia (see Table C1 over page), useful books and web sites providing valuable information for parents. The *Raising Children Network* web site has a comprehensive list of services and resources available for parents (https://raisingchildren.net.au/grown-ups/services-support/services-families/parent-family-services).

Useful books

- *Parenting through the storm* (Ann Douglas).

- *Nurturing young minds: Mental wellbeing in the digital age. Generation next* (Dr Ramesh Manocha [Ed.])

- *Growing happy, healthy young minds. Generation next* (Dr Ramesh Manocha [Ed.])

- *Staying connected to your teenager. How to keep them talking to you and how to hear what they're really saying* (Michael Riera).

- *Surviving adolescents 2.0* (Michael Carr-Gregg & Elly Robinson).

- *Tricky teens* (Andrew Fuller).

Table C1 Evidence-based parenting programs available in Australia

Program name	Contact details
Parent Effectiveness Training	http://parenteffectivenesstraining.net.au/ Look for instructors in your state or territory.
Resourceful Adolescent Program	www.rap.qut.edu.au This web site provides information about the course and training, although not people who run the courses.
Tuning in to Teens	www.tuningintokids.org.au This web site is about the kids program but also includes information about the teens program. It includes a calendar of program events for parents.
Parenting Adolescents: A Creative Experience (PACE)	No web site currently available but look out for this course if it is offered in your community.
Triple P Parenting programs for parents of teens	www.triplep-parenting.net.au/au-uken/get-started/triple-p-courses-for-parents-of-teens/ Website includes information about the courses, a search function to find a course in your local area as well as information about an online course.
Parentworks	https://parentworks.org.au/#/ An online parenting program for parents of children aged 2 to 16 years.
ReachOut Parents	https://parents.au.reachout.com/ Online resource, including a coaching service for parents of teenagers.

- *Be a parent not a pal* (Dr Jeff Kemp).

- *Parenting troubled teens* (Z. Ong).

- *Inventing ourselves. The secret life of the teenage brain* (Sarah-Jayne Blakemore).

- *How to talk so teens will listen and listen so teens will talk* (Adele Faber & Elaine Mazlish).

- *The reflective parent* (Regina Pally).

- *Emotionally intelligent parenting* (M. Elias, S.E. Tobias & B.S. Friedlander).

- *Parenting teenagers* (The Reach Foundation).

- *Healing self-injury: A compassionate guide for parents and other loved ones* (Janis Whitlock and Elizabeth Lloyd-Richardson).

- *Self harm. Why teens do it and what parents can do to help* (Michelle Mitchell).

Web sites

- Cybersmart (www.cybersmart.gov.au), Australian Communications and Media Authority — designed to help children and whole families find out how to be cybersmart and use the internet safely.

- The Kids Are All Right (www.thekidsareallright.com.au/category/technology/) — designed for parents of teenagers and includes a blog with a special section on technology.

- Raising Children's Network (https://raisingchildren.net.au/).

- Office of the ESafety Commissioner (www.esafety.gov.au/).

- Reachout Parents (https://parents.au.reachout.com/).